A Very Happy Meowy Christmas

Coloring Book

Printed in the United States of America

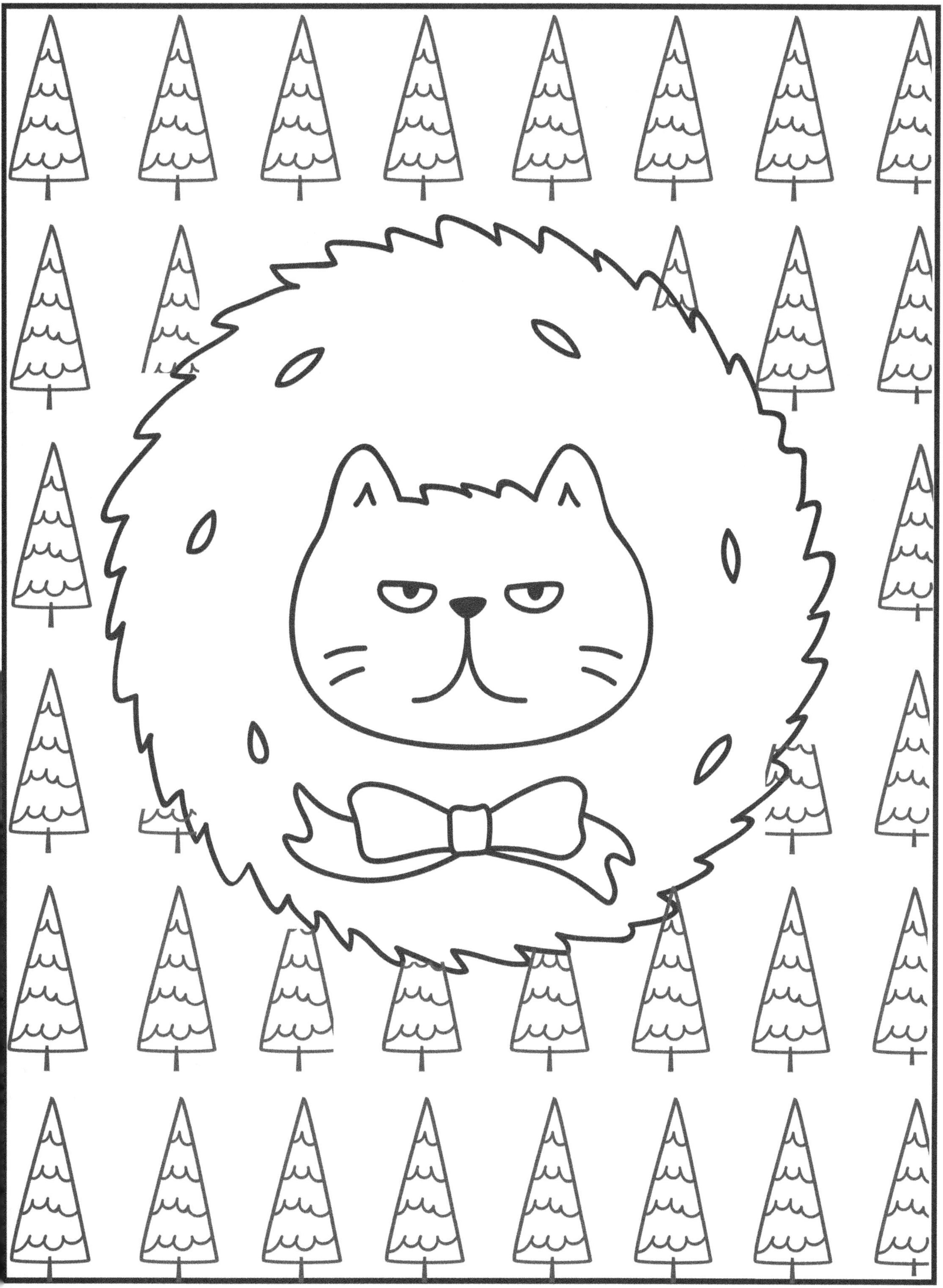

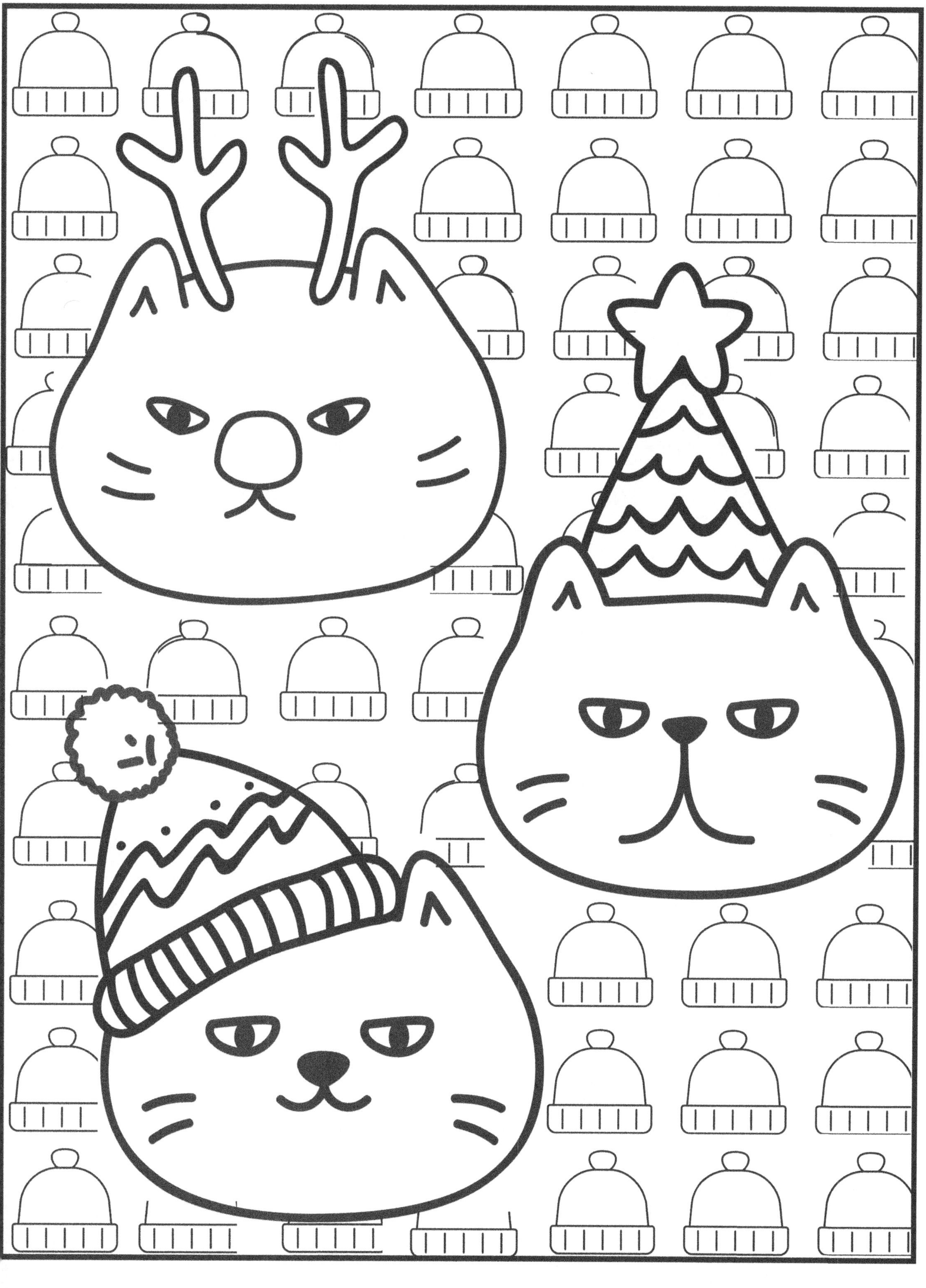

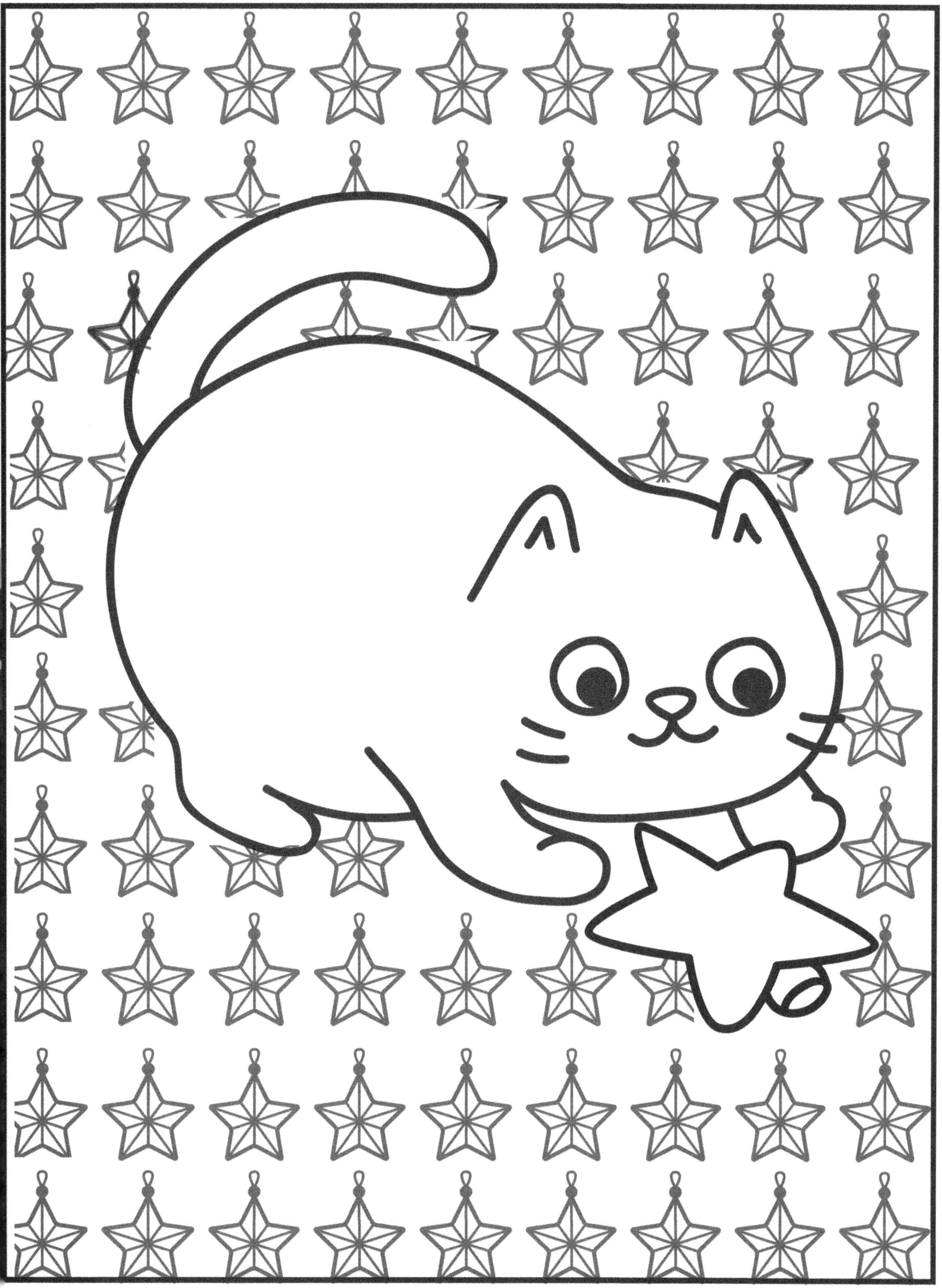

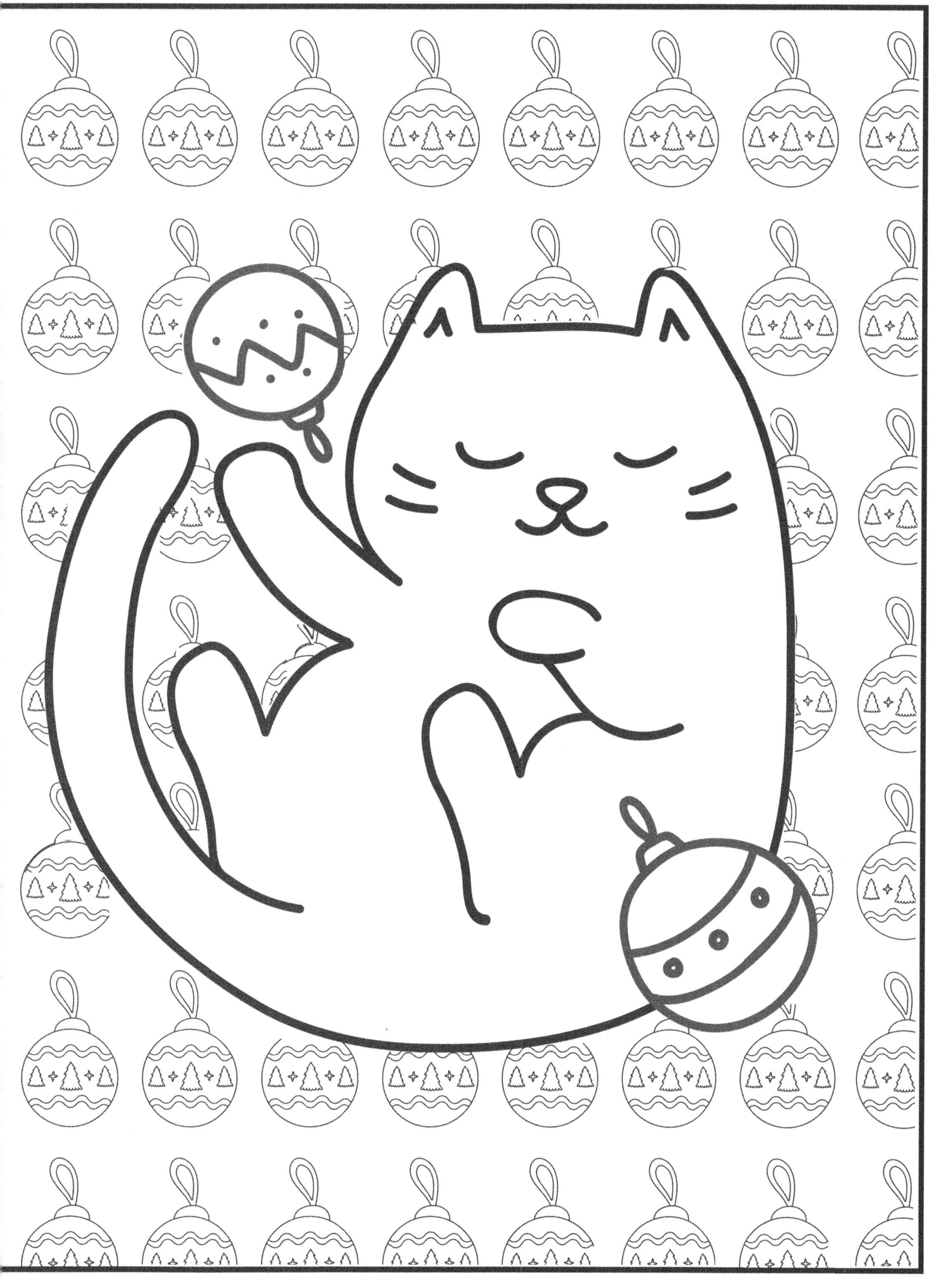

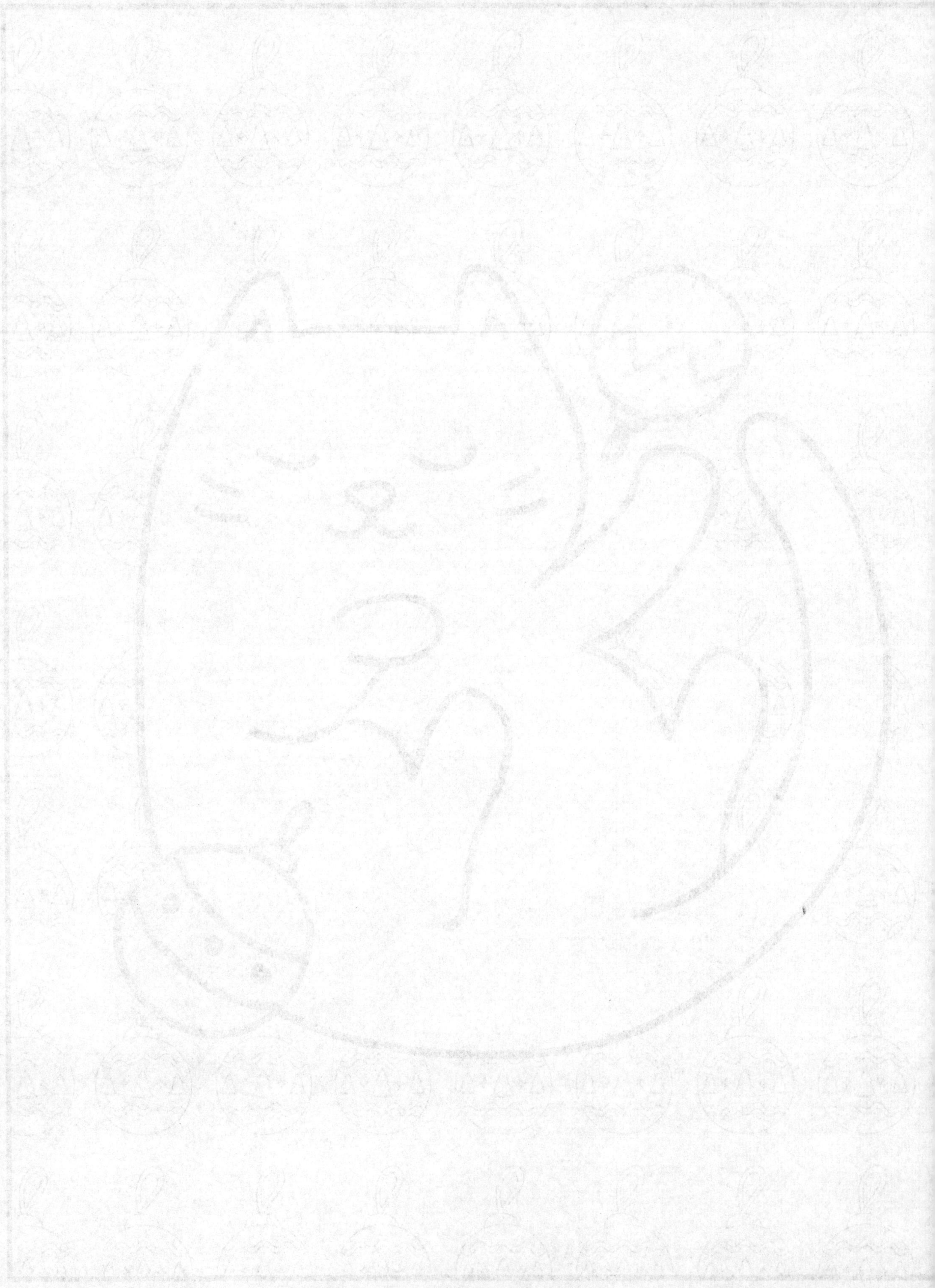

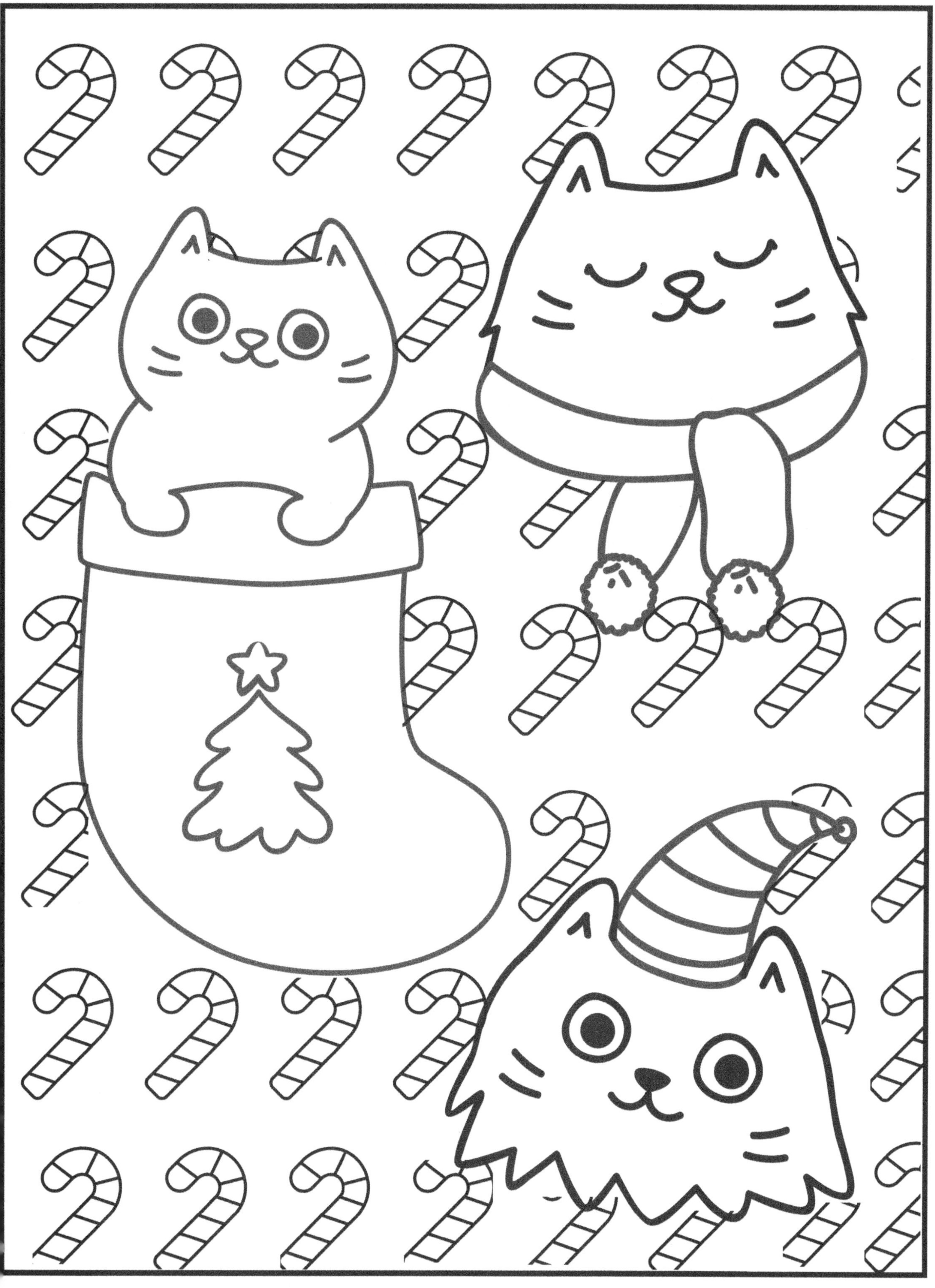

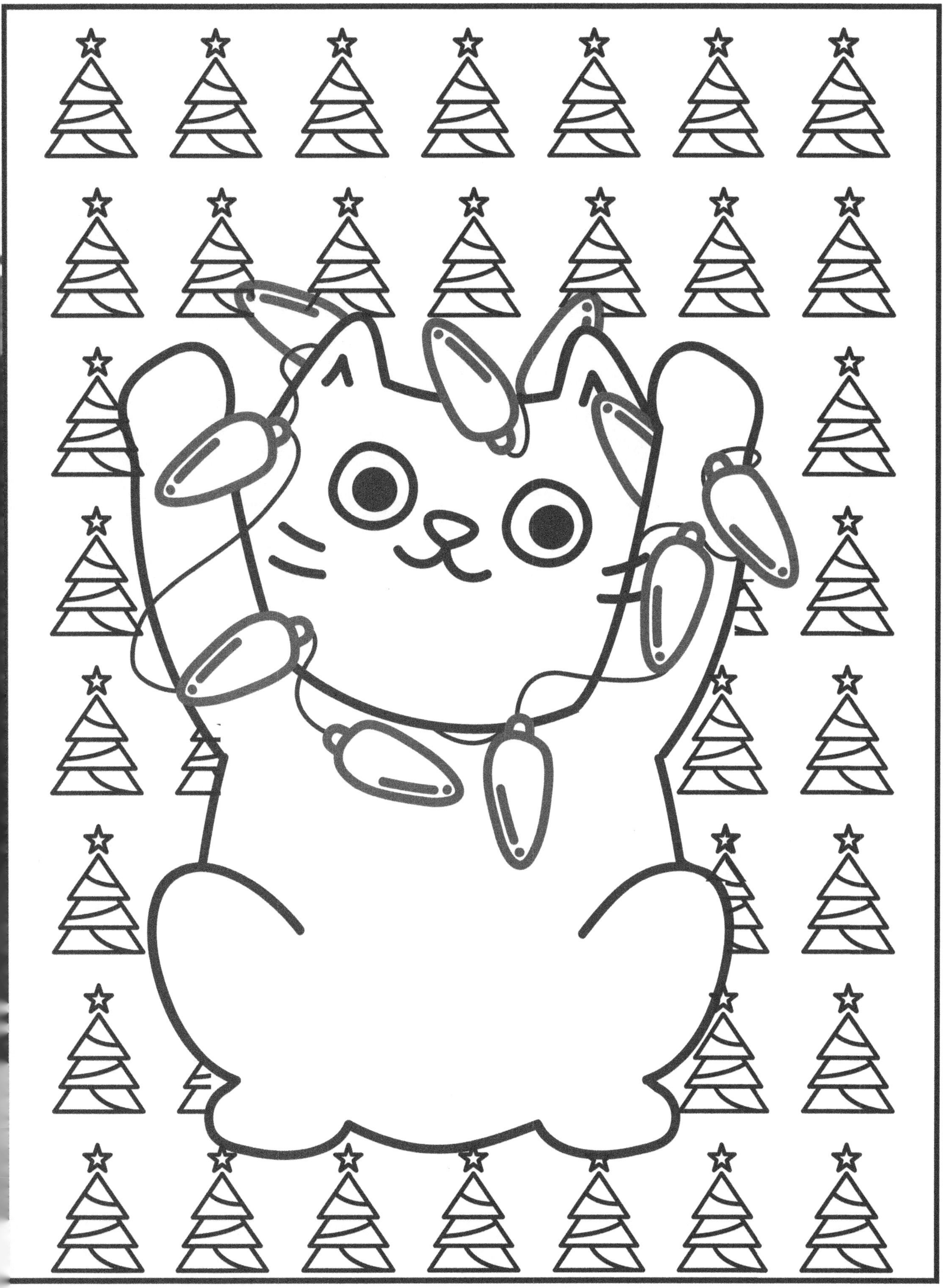

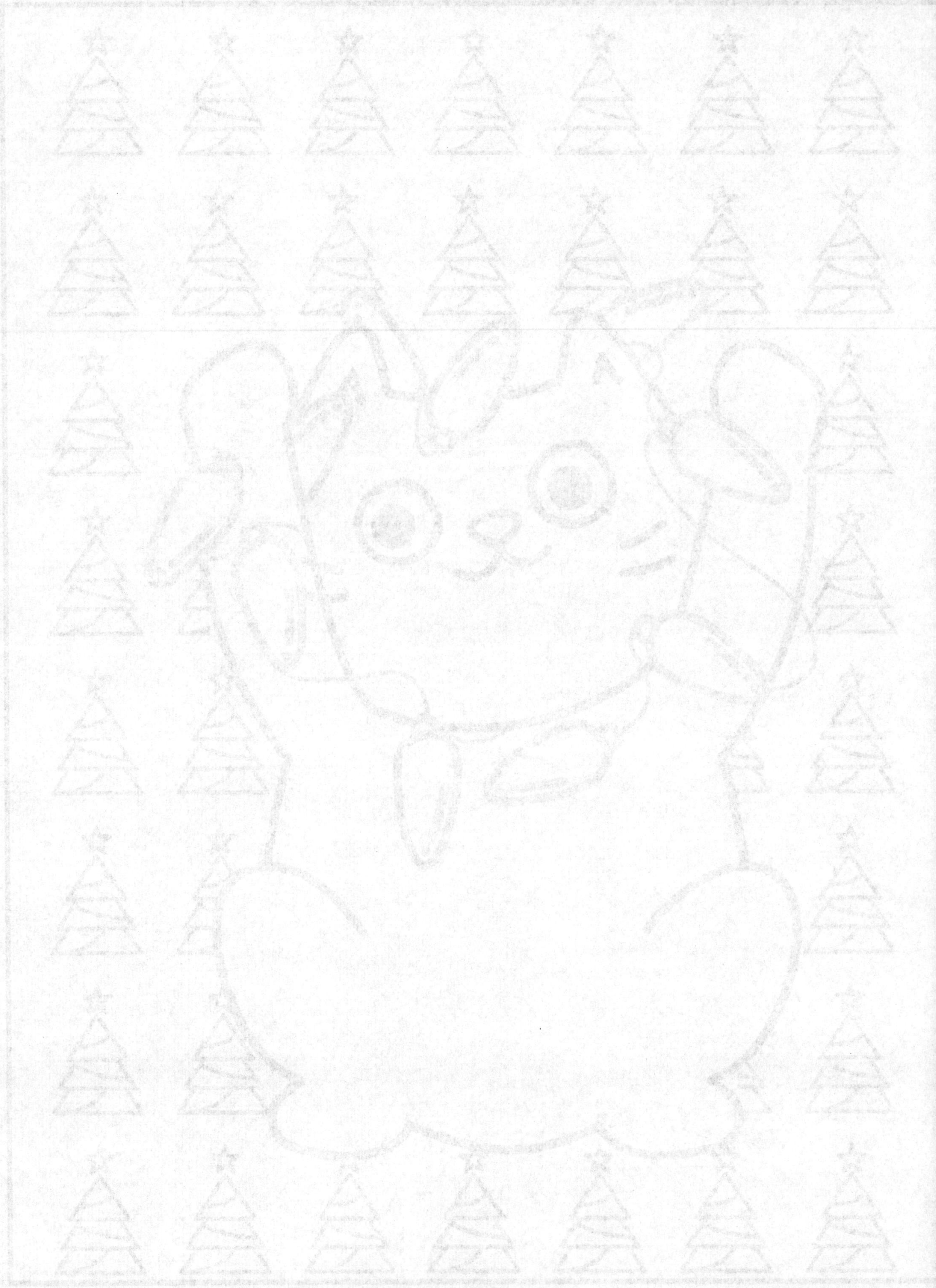

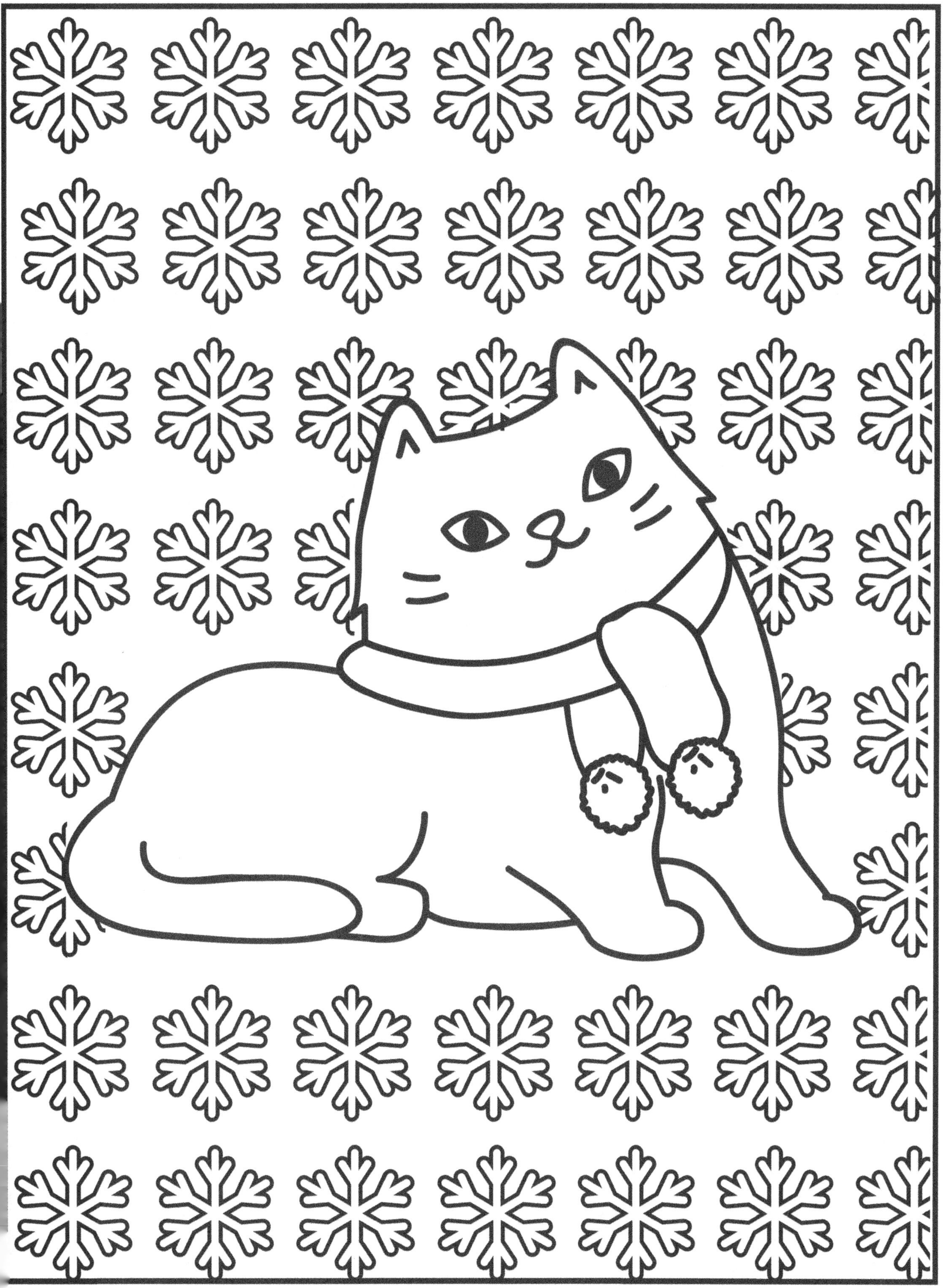

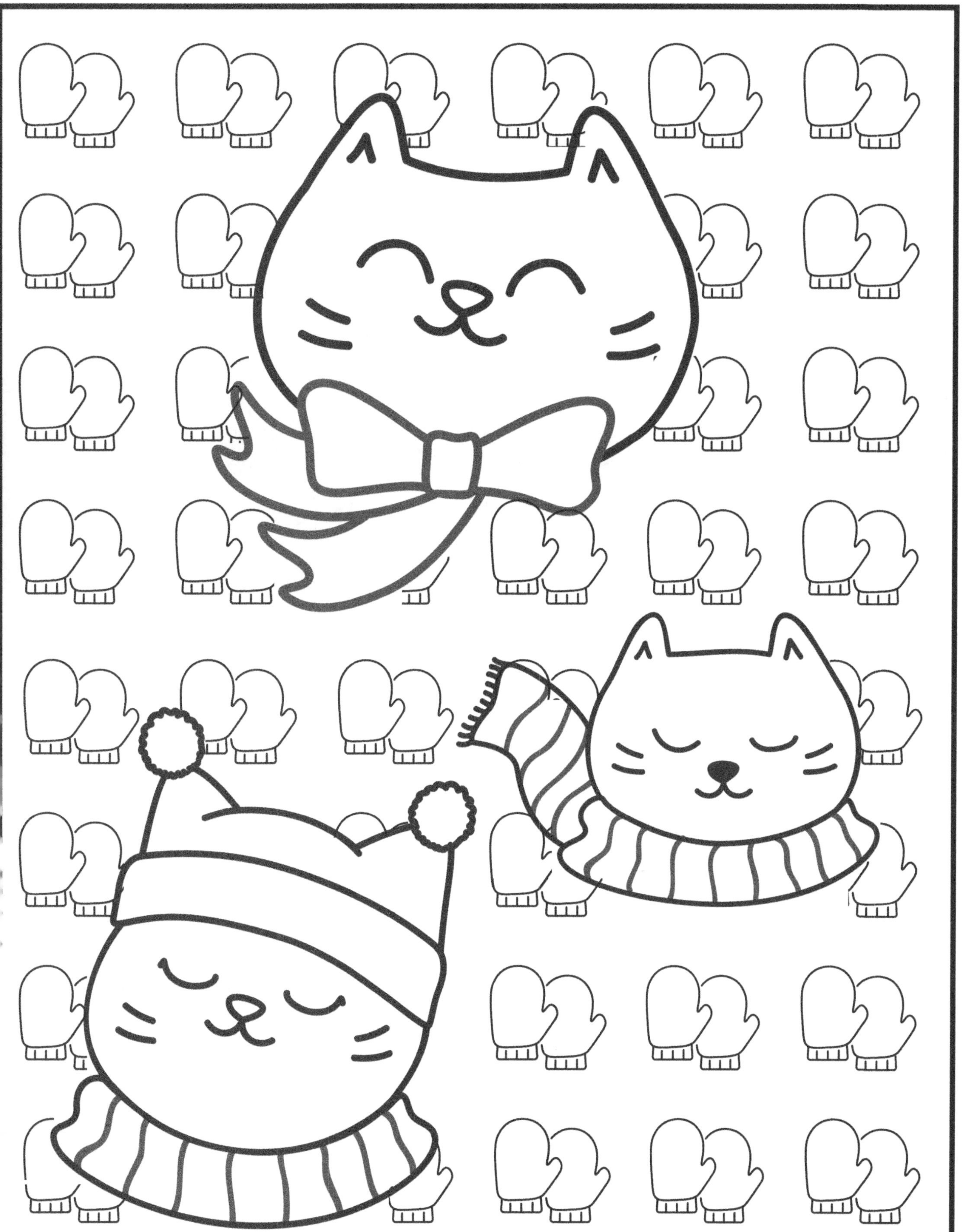

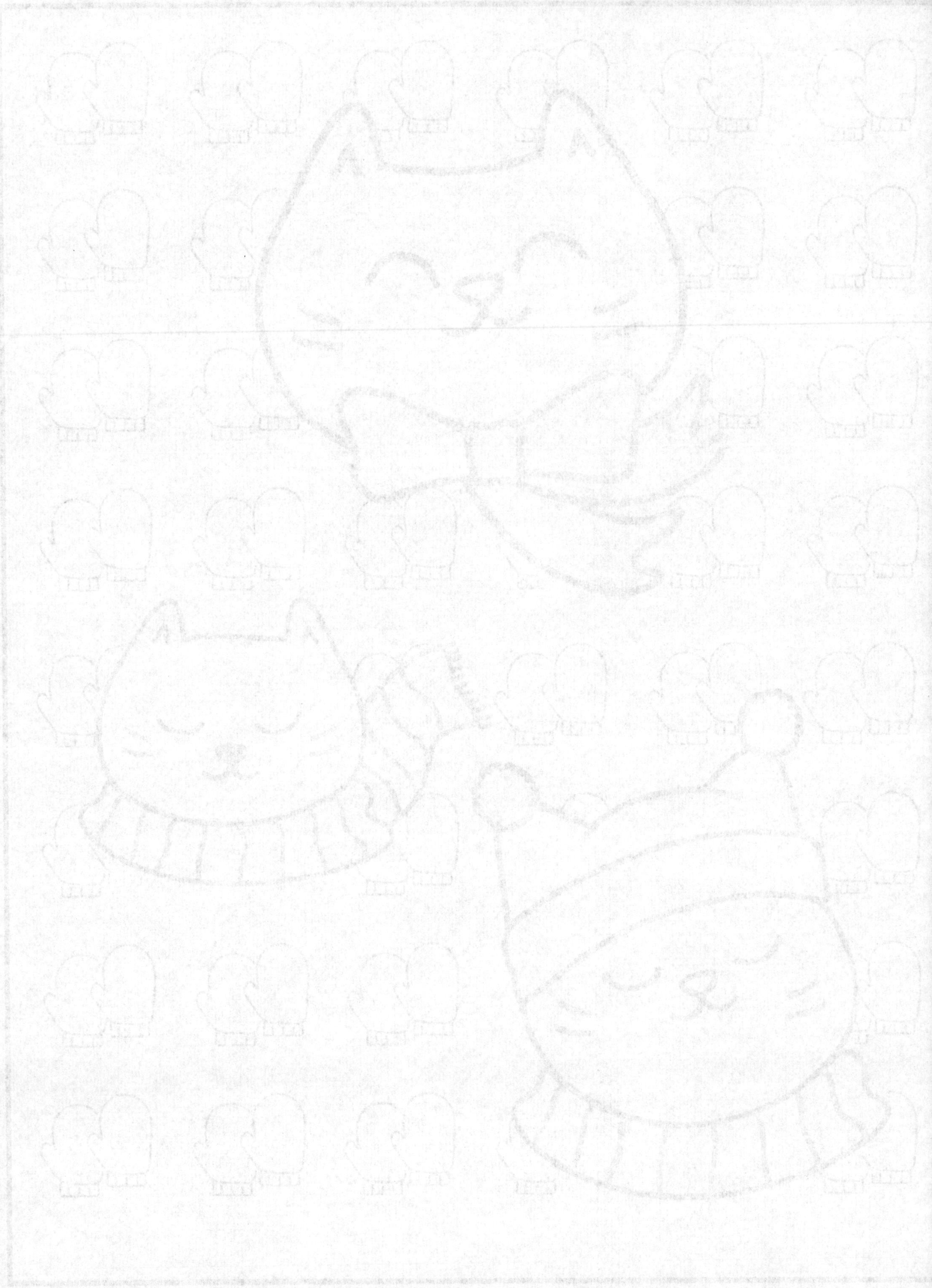

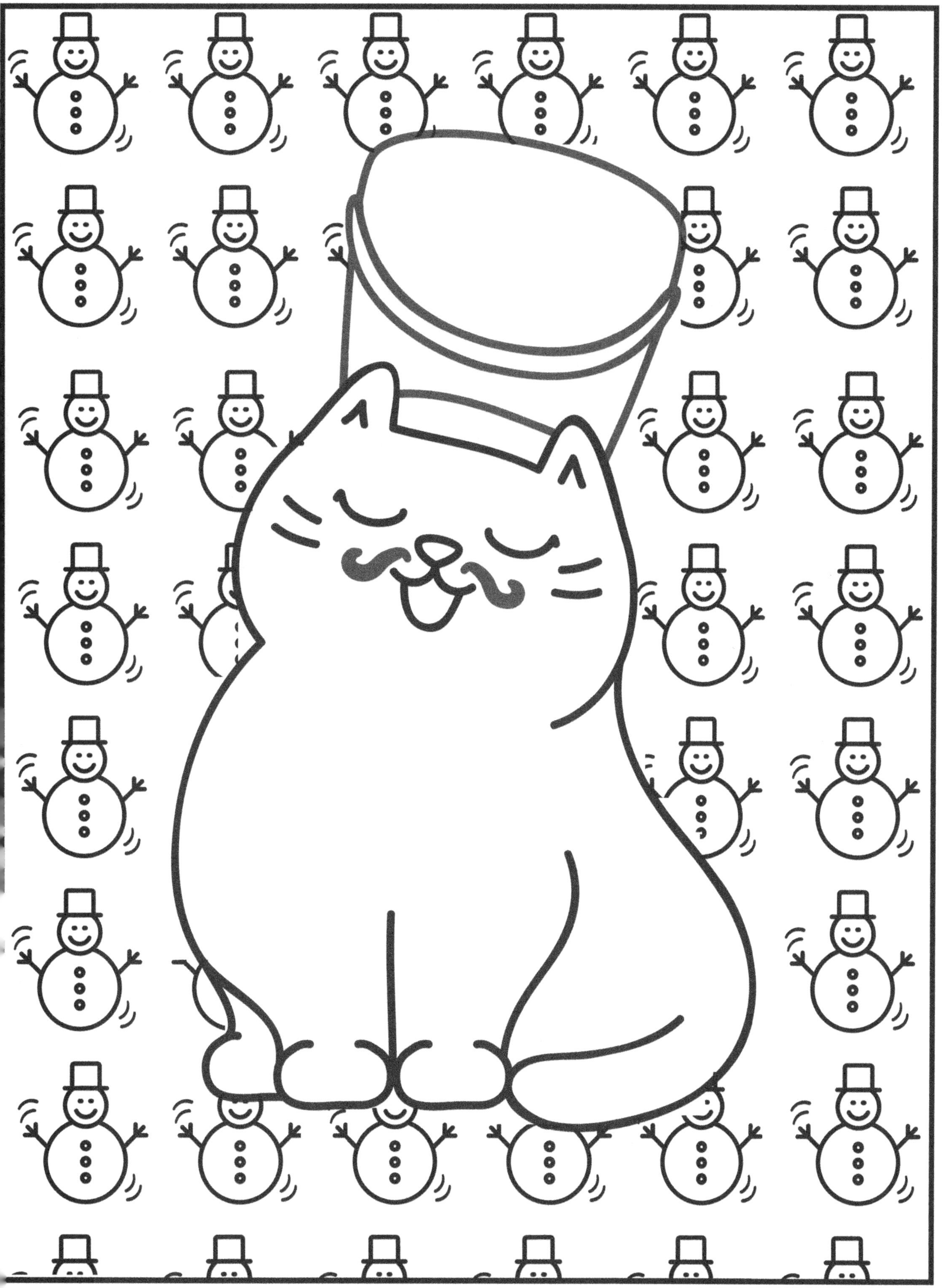

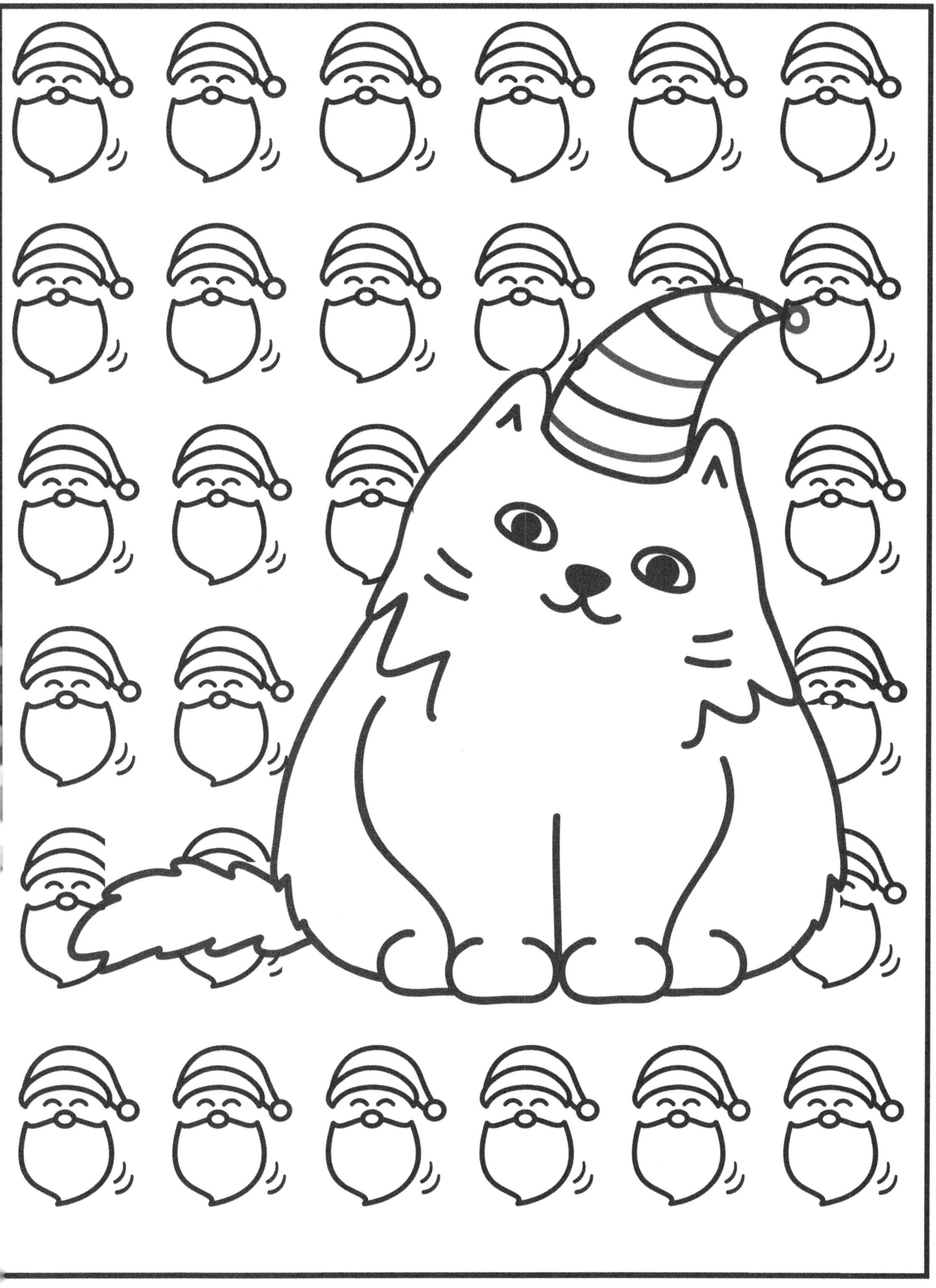

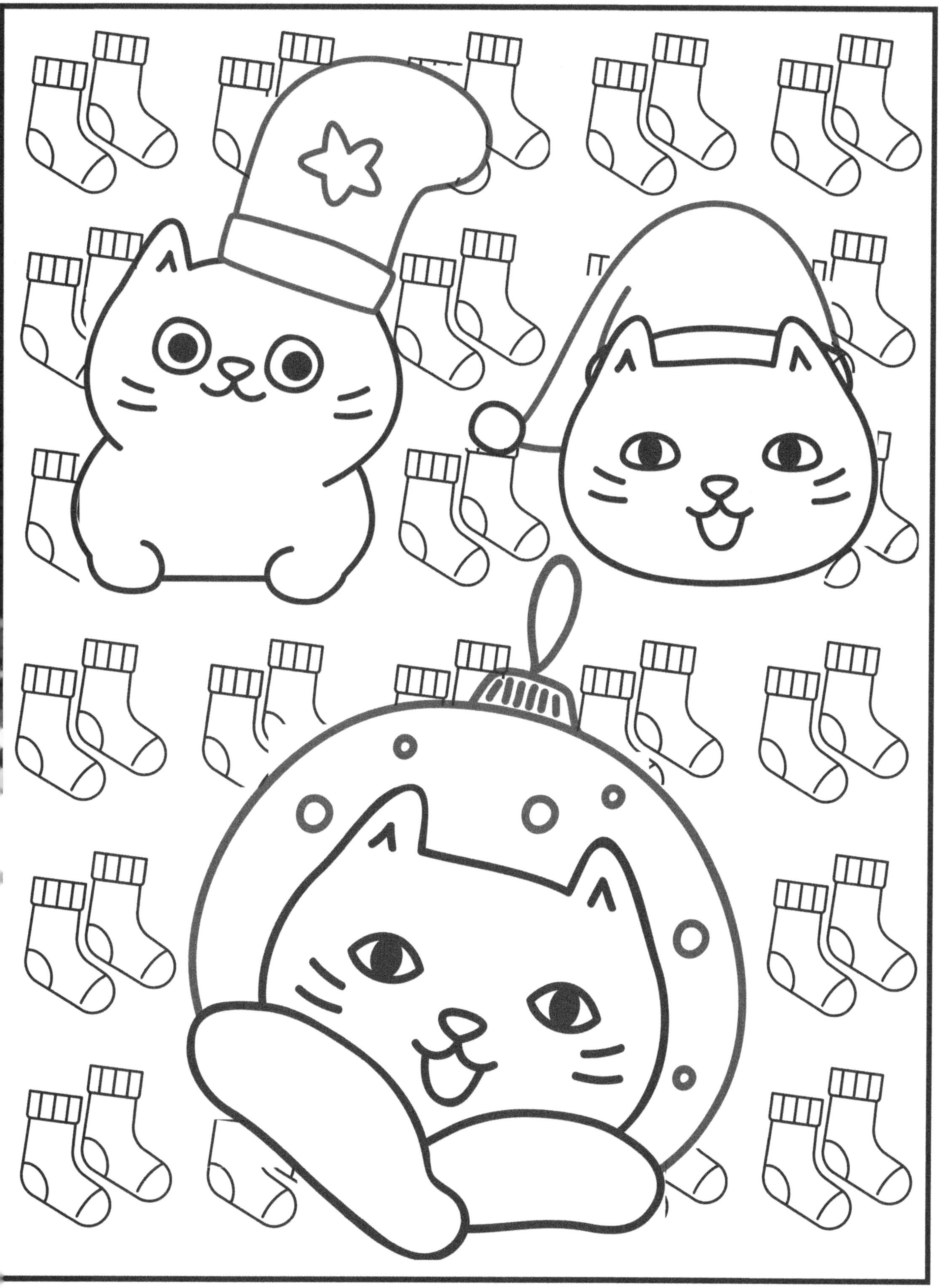

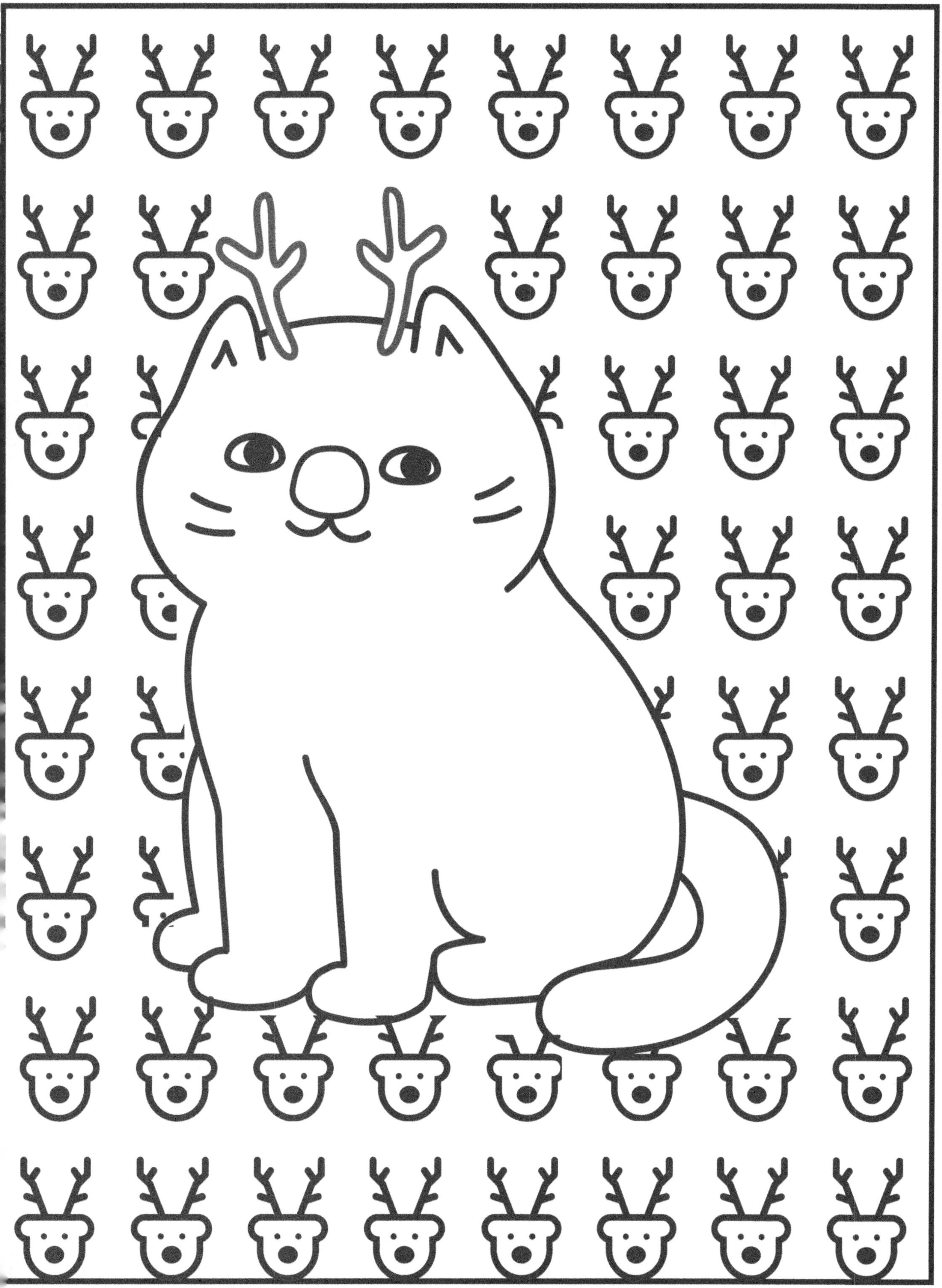

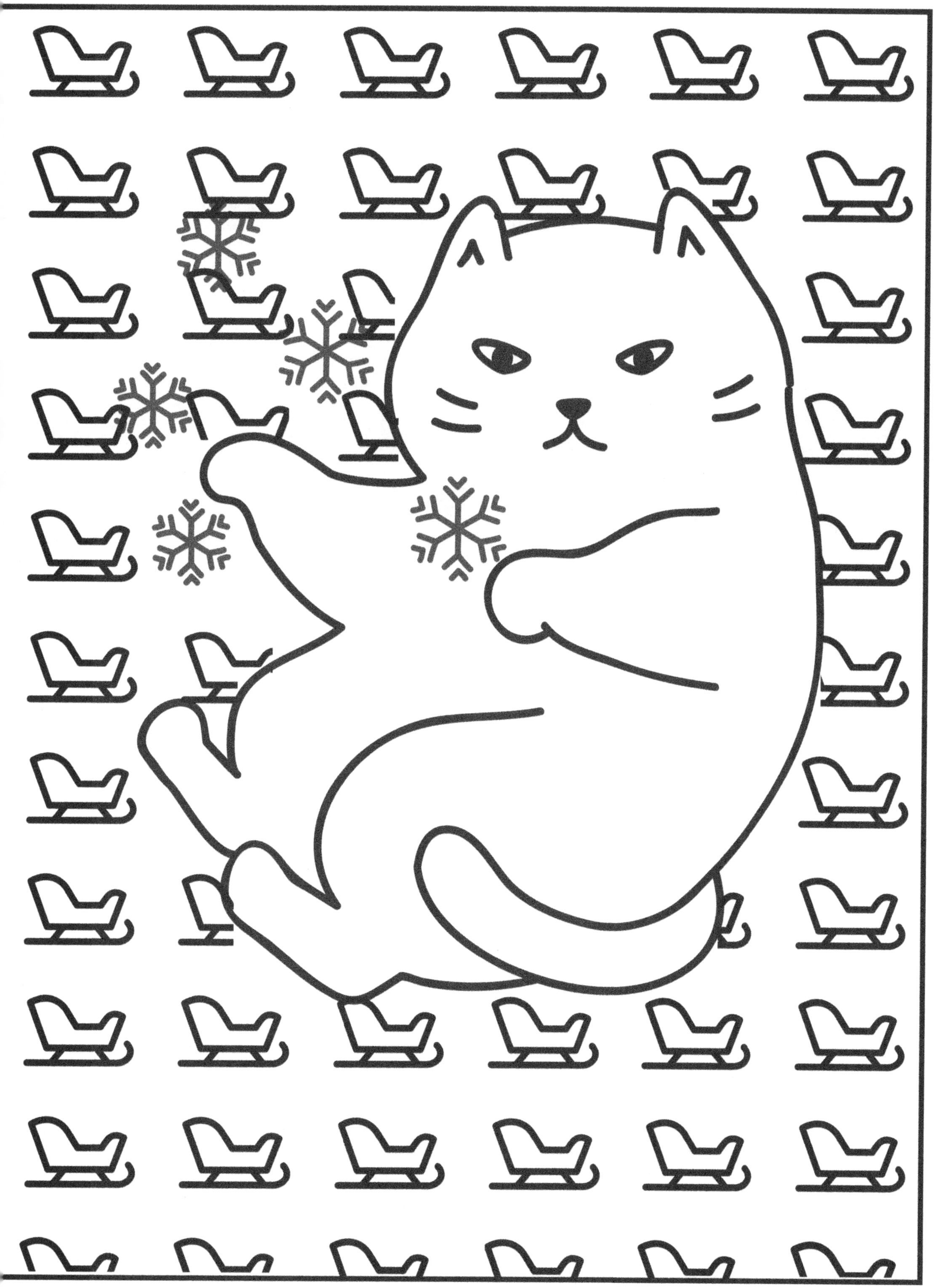

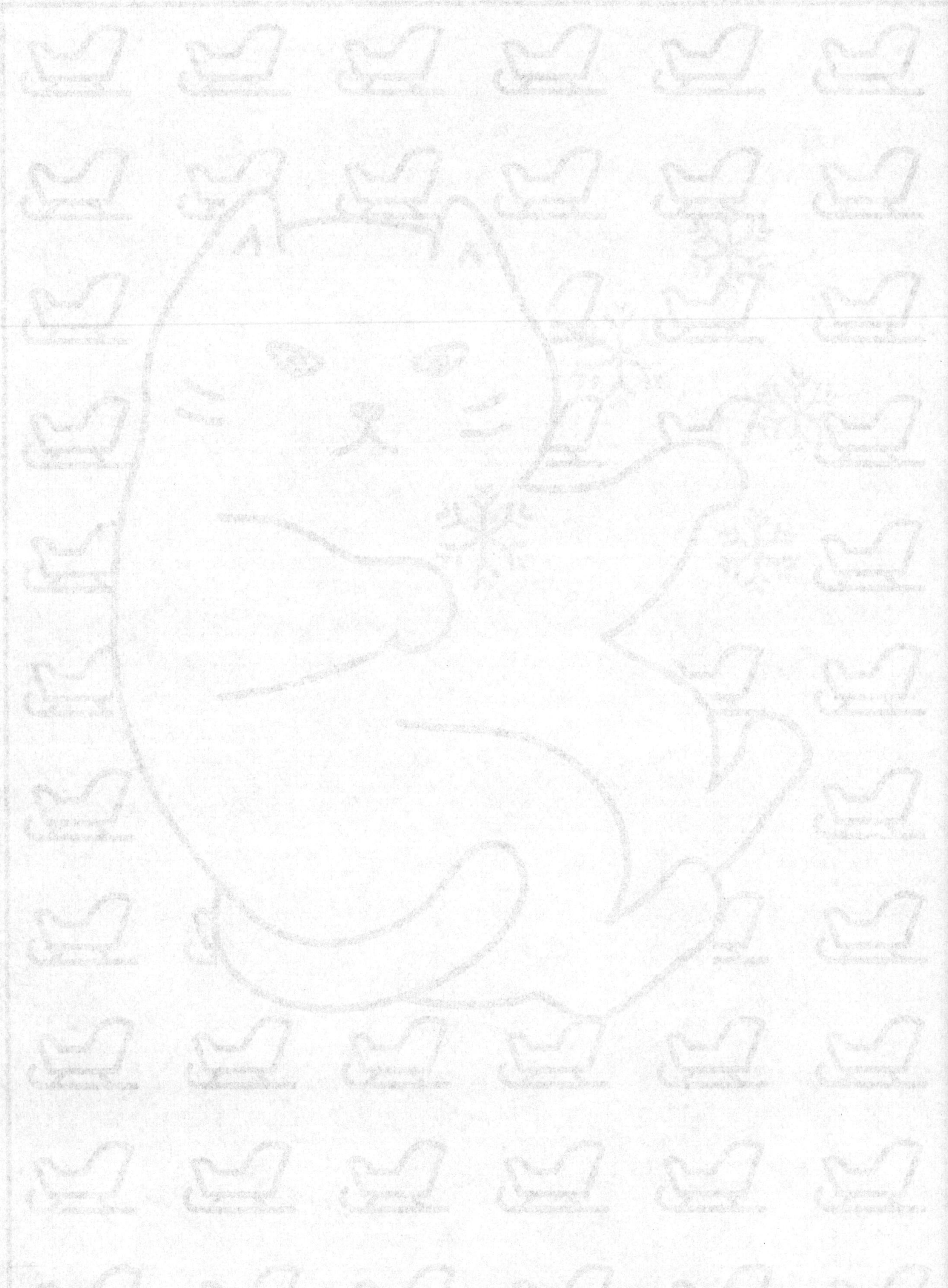

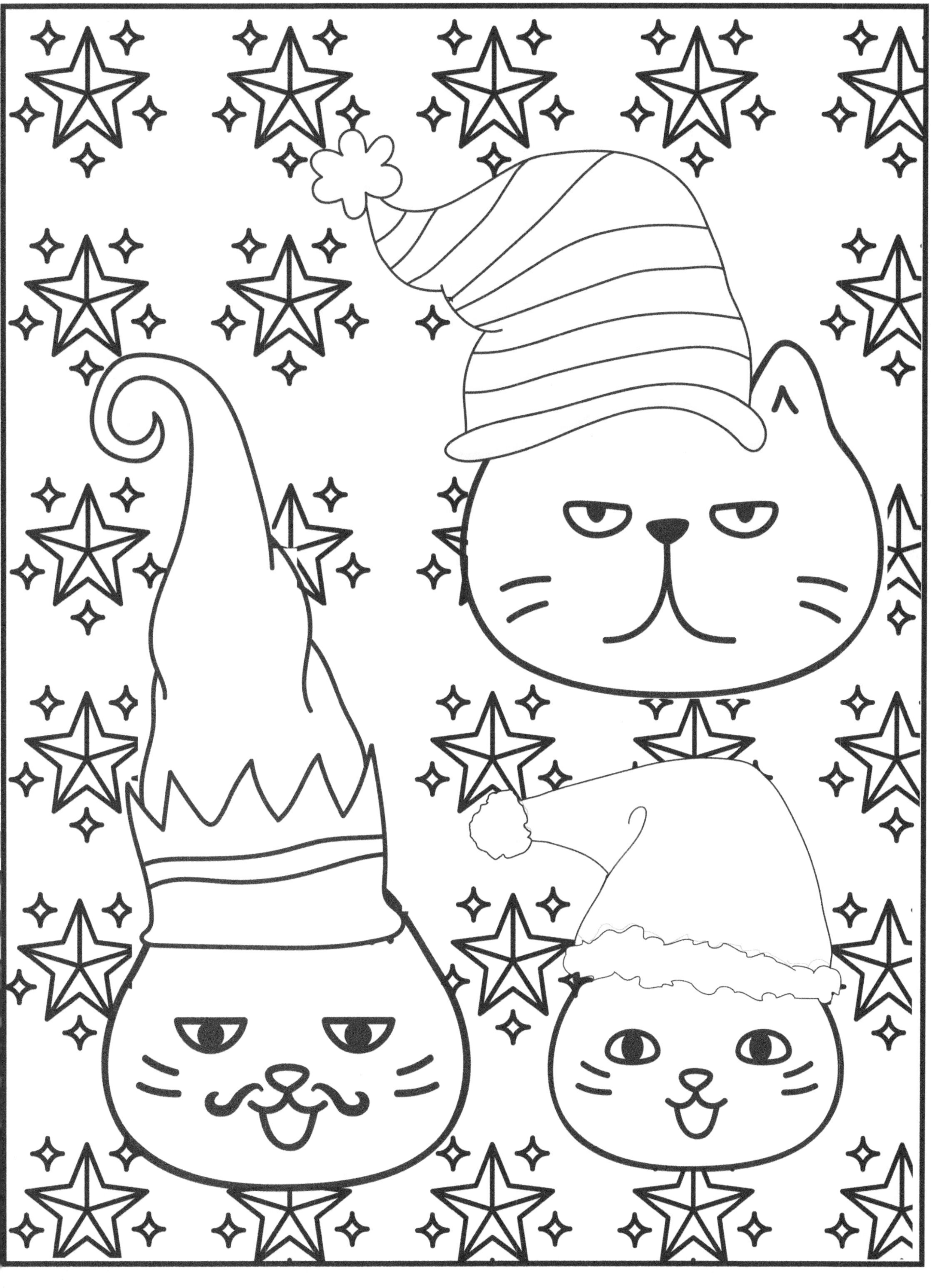

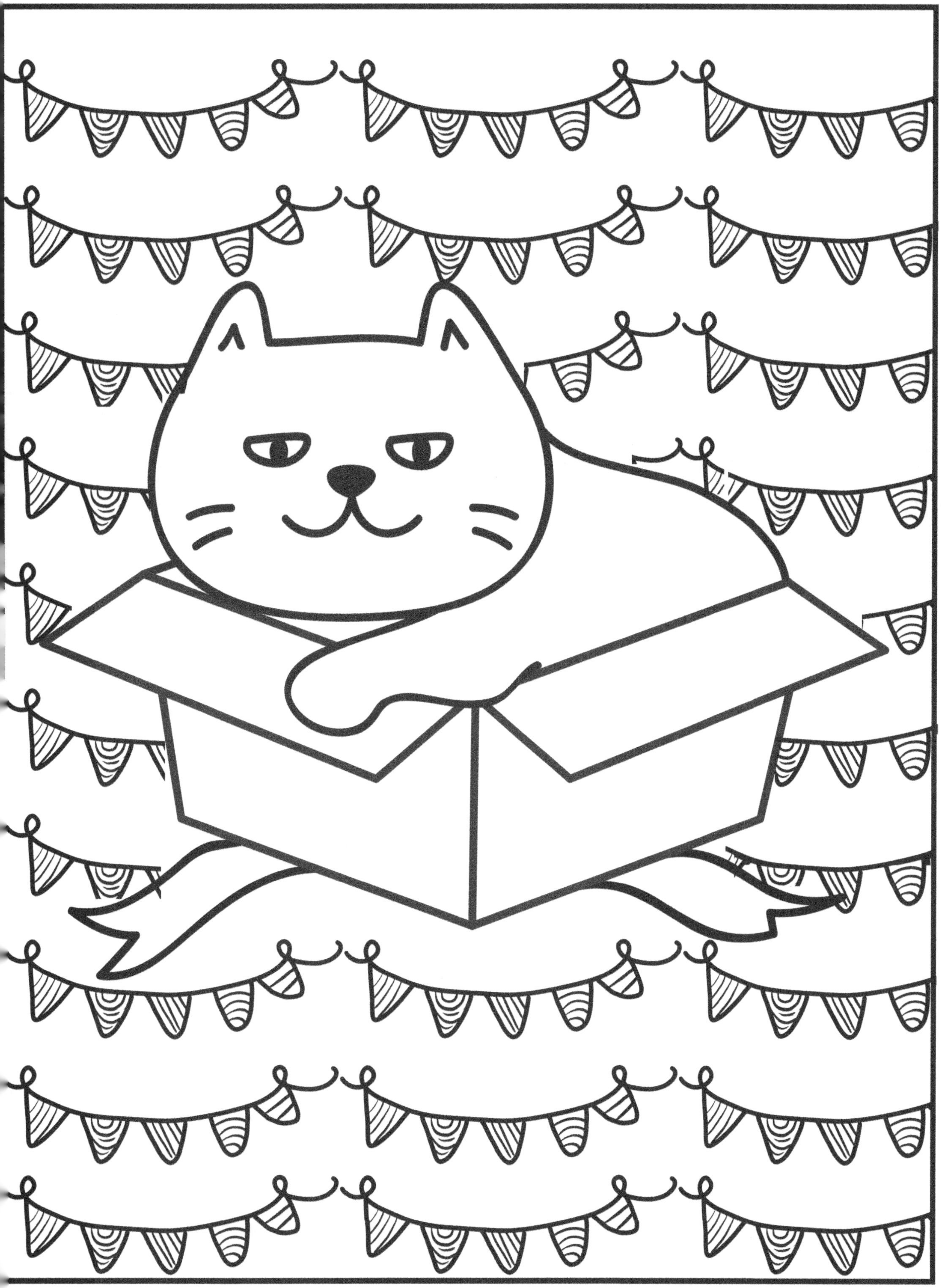

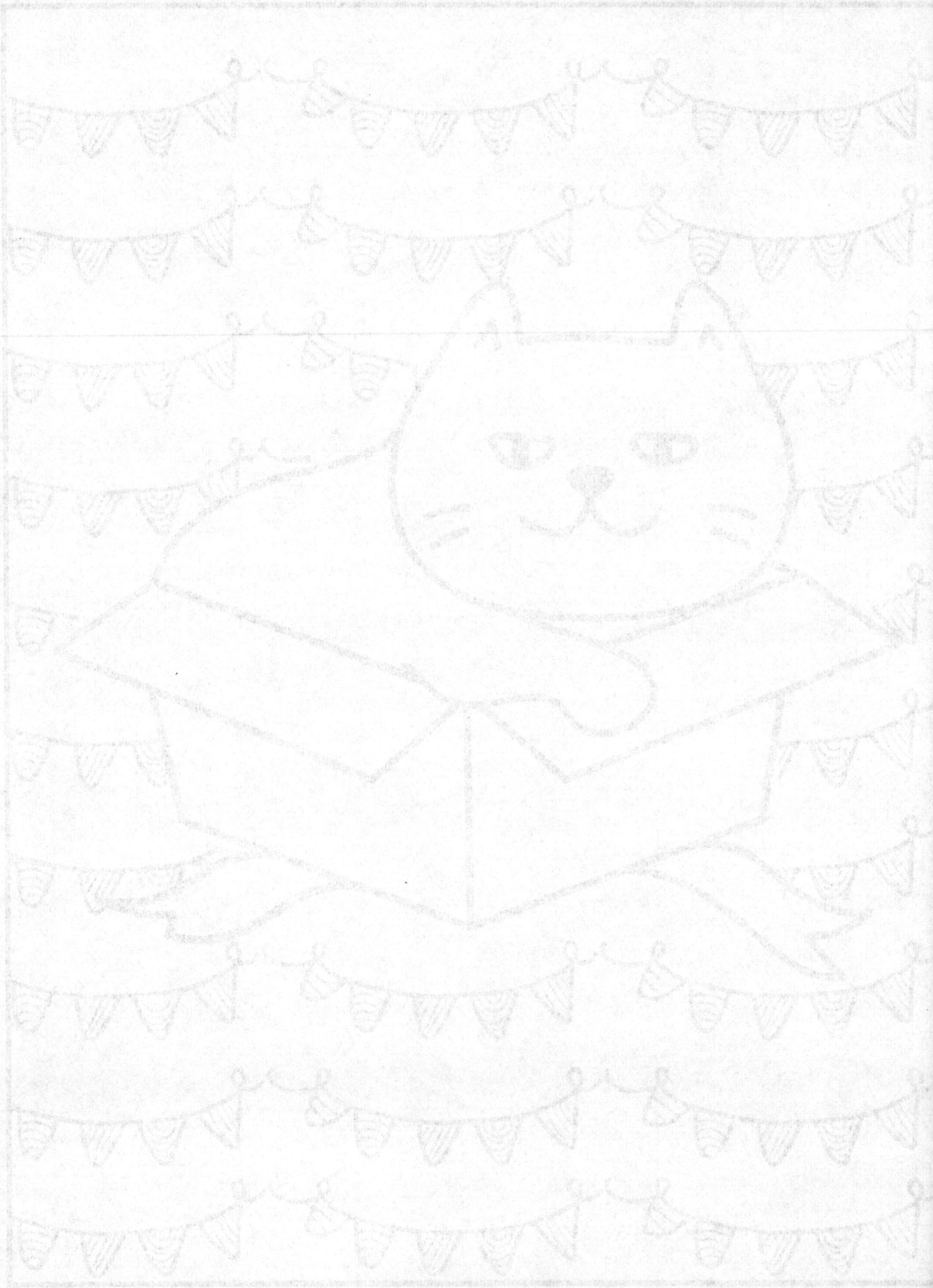

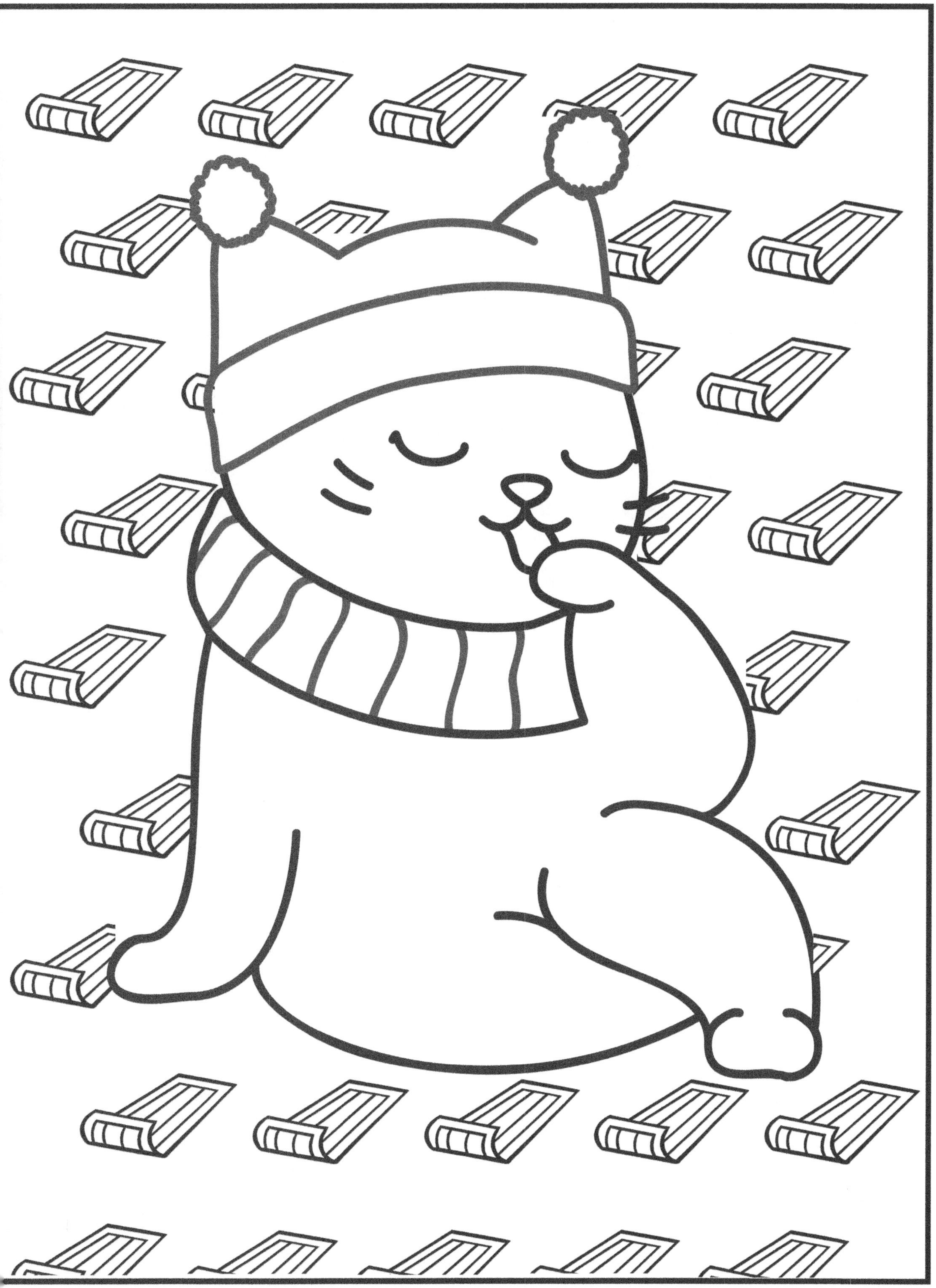

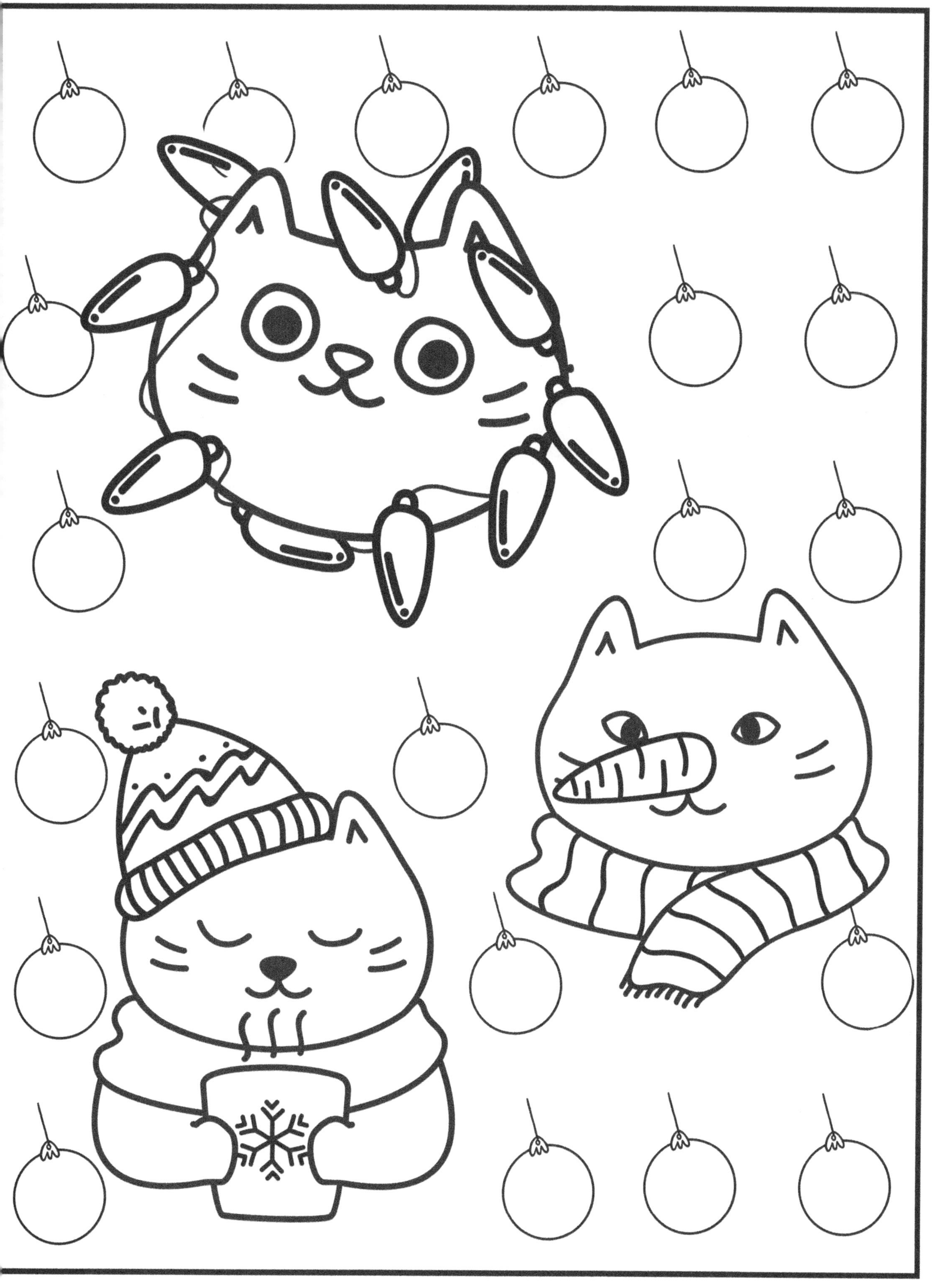

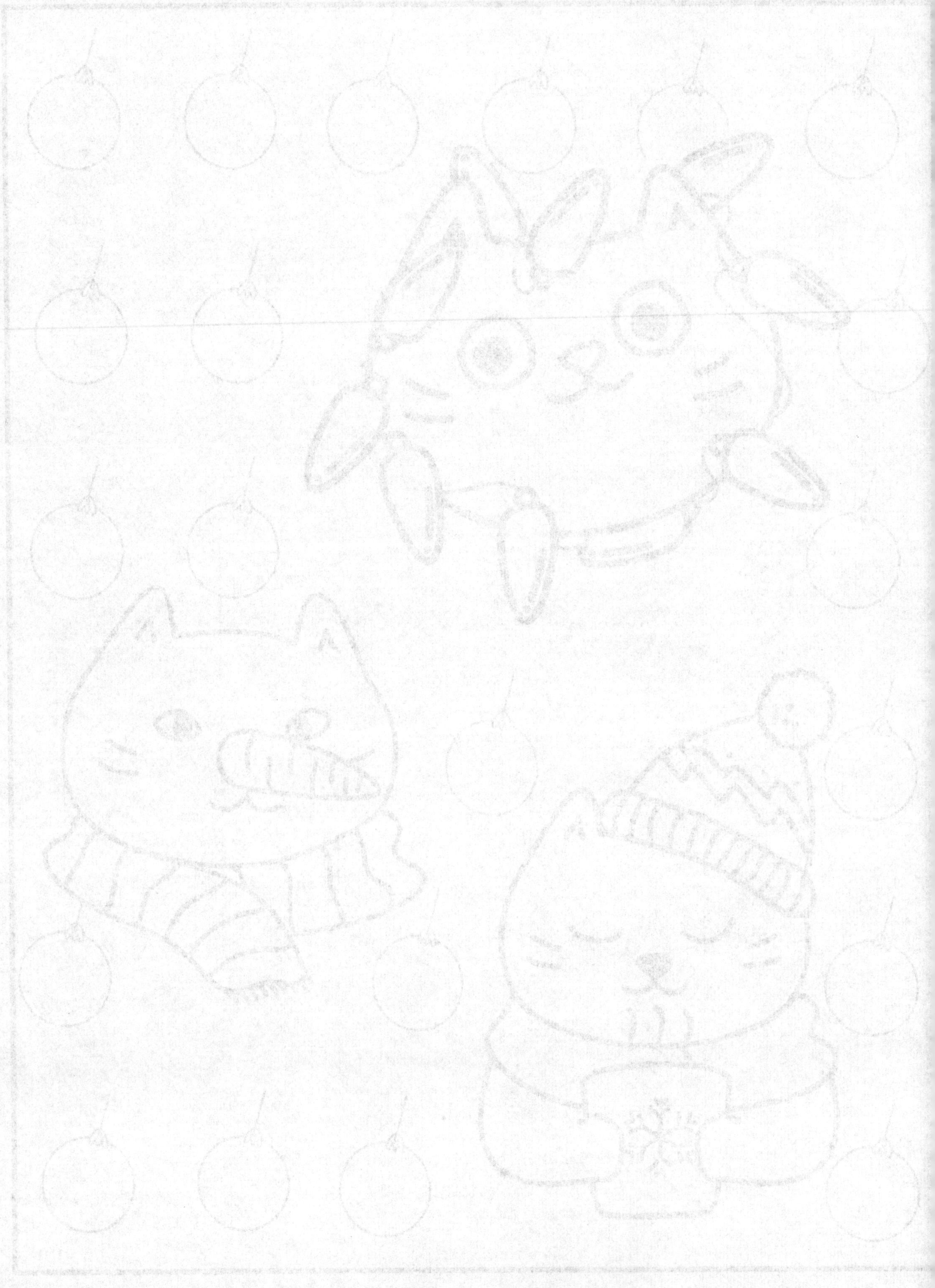

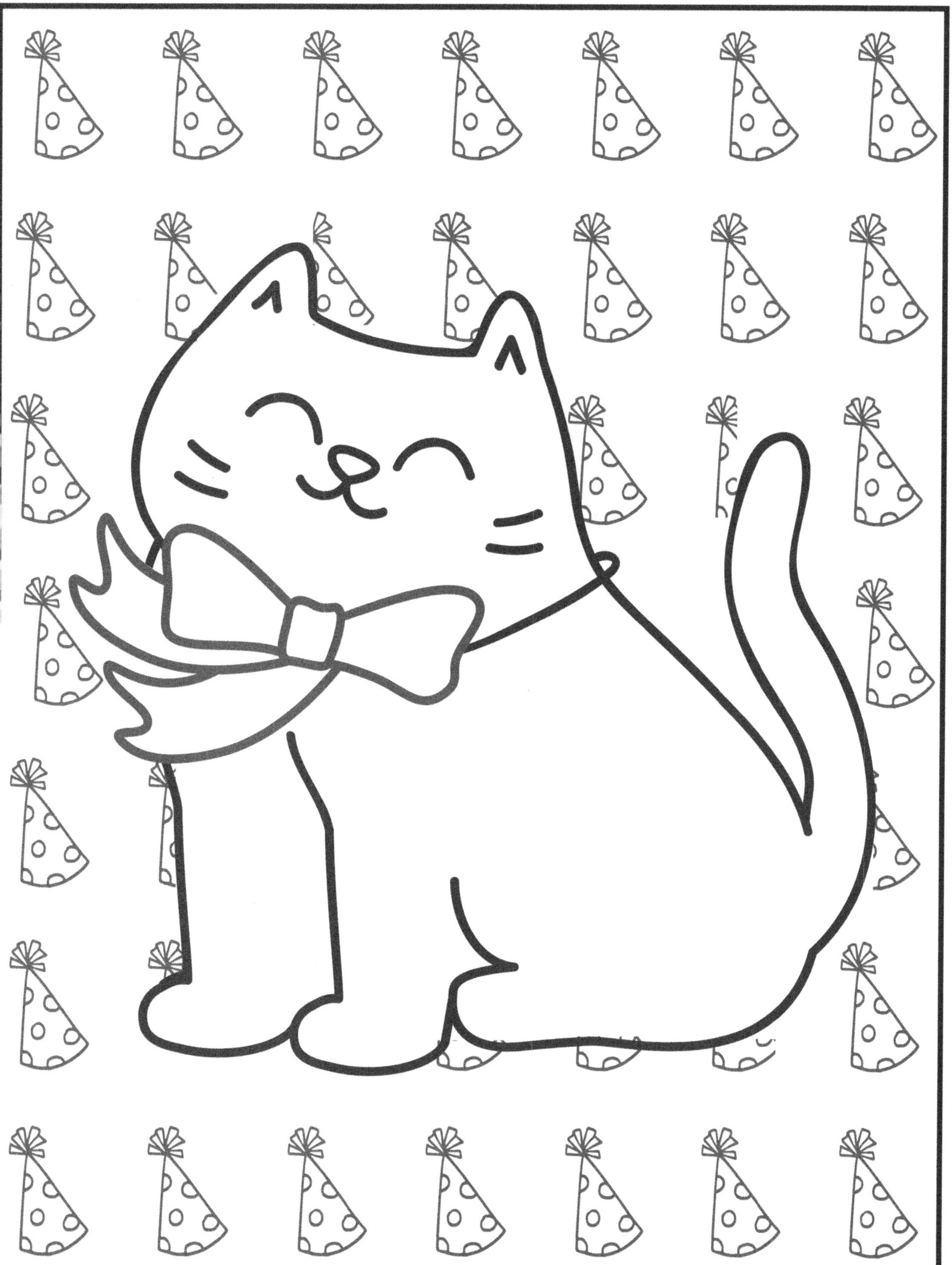

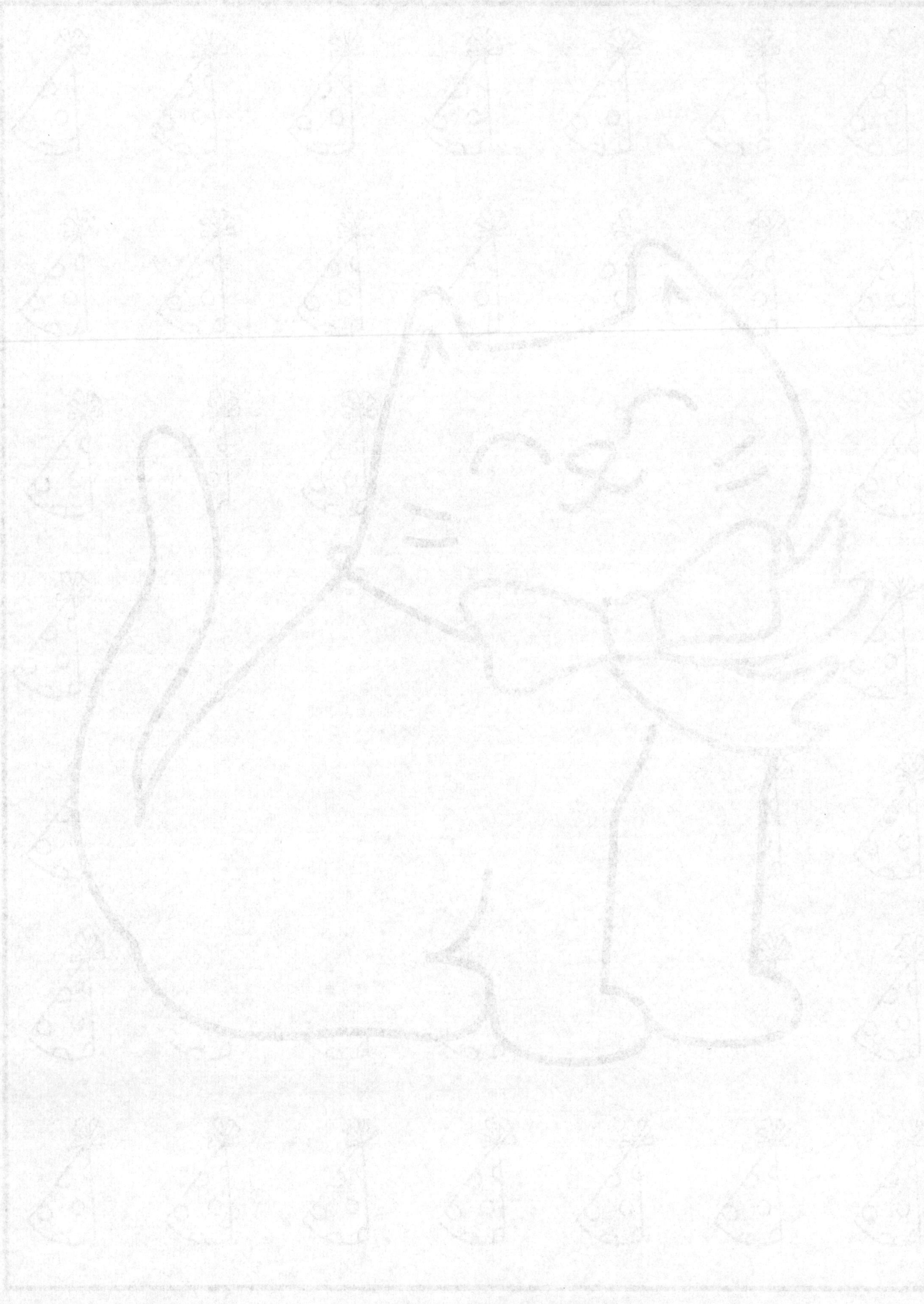

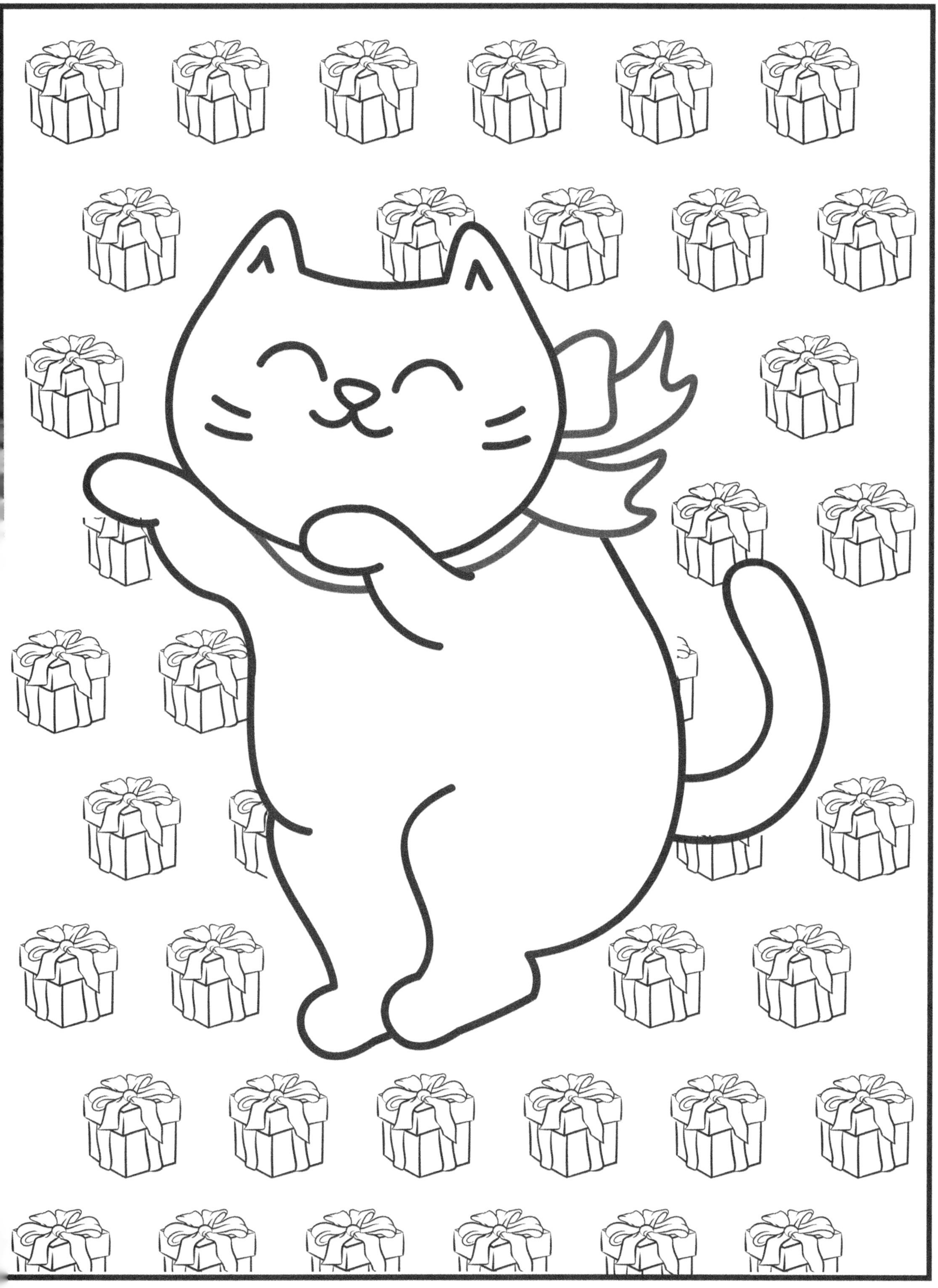

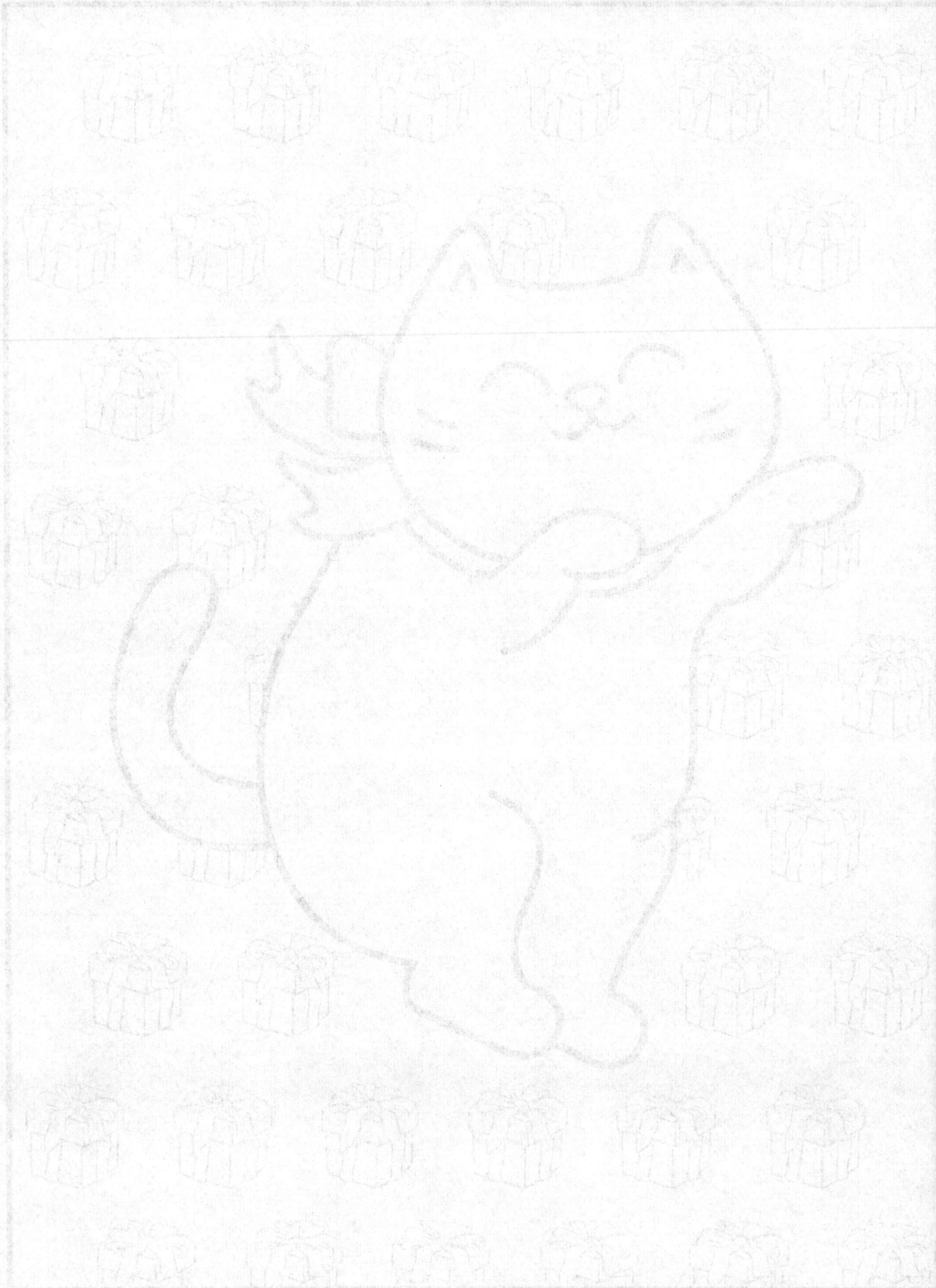

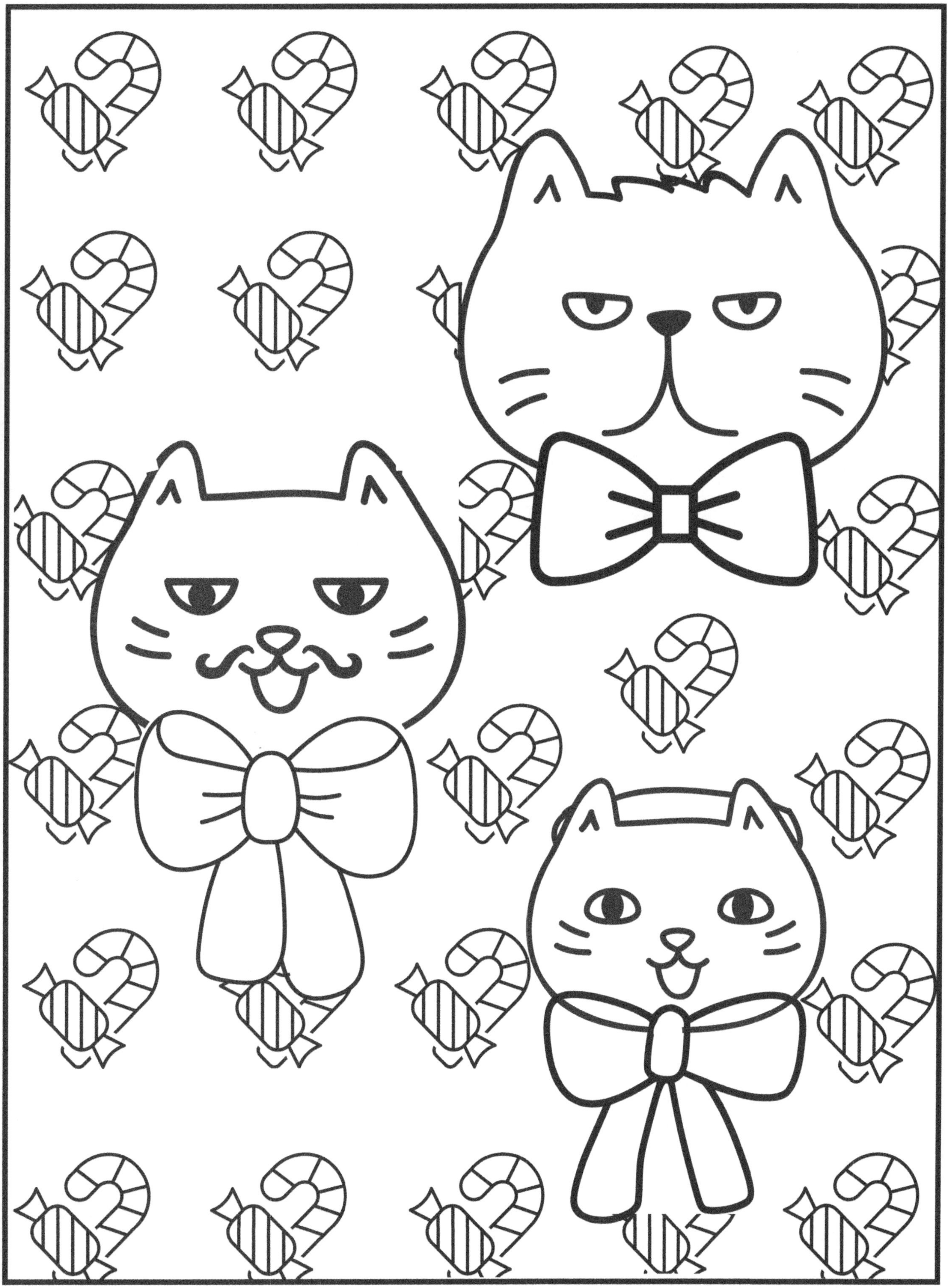

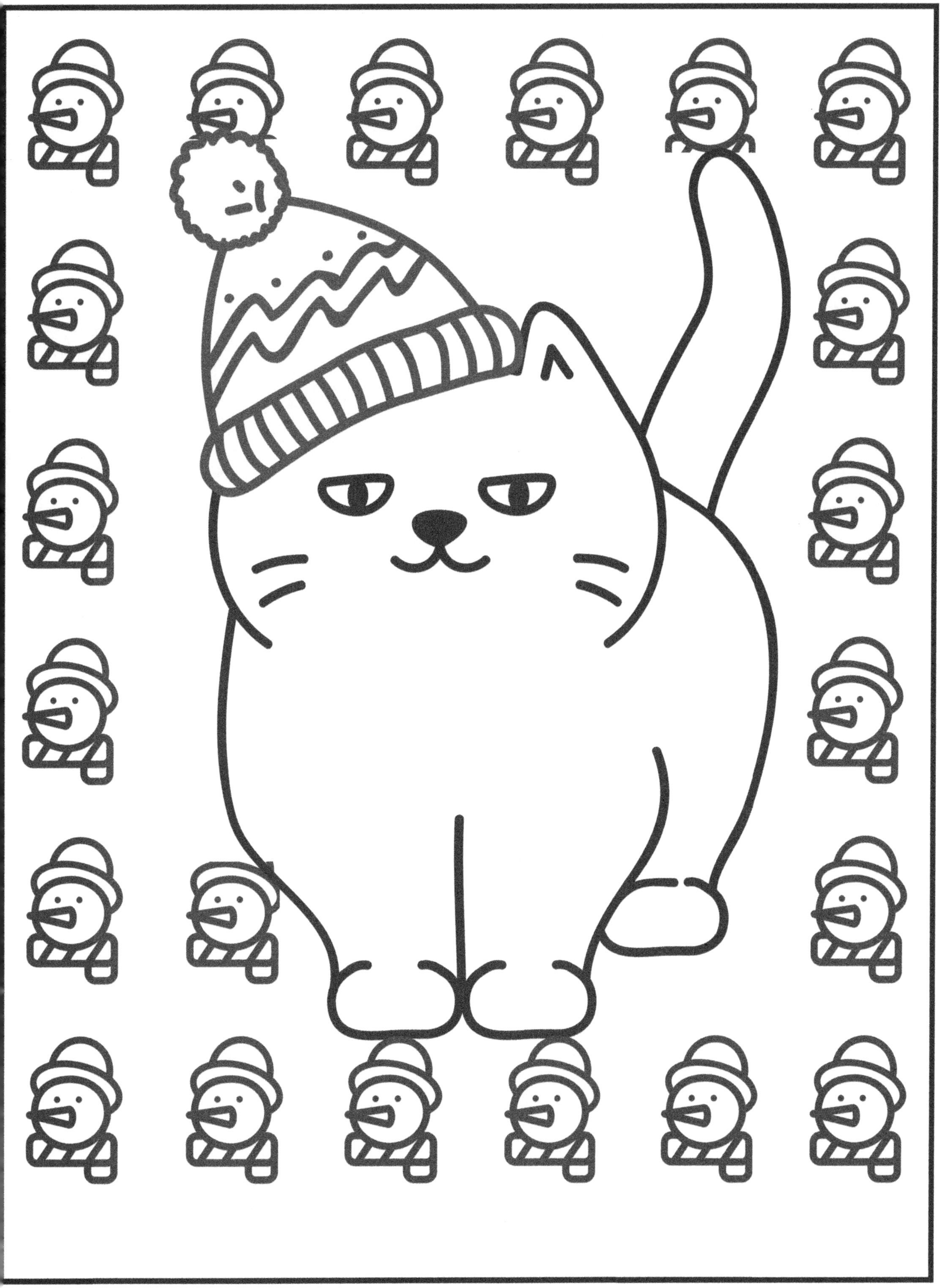

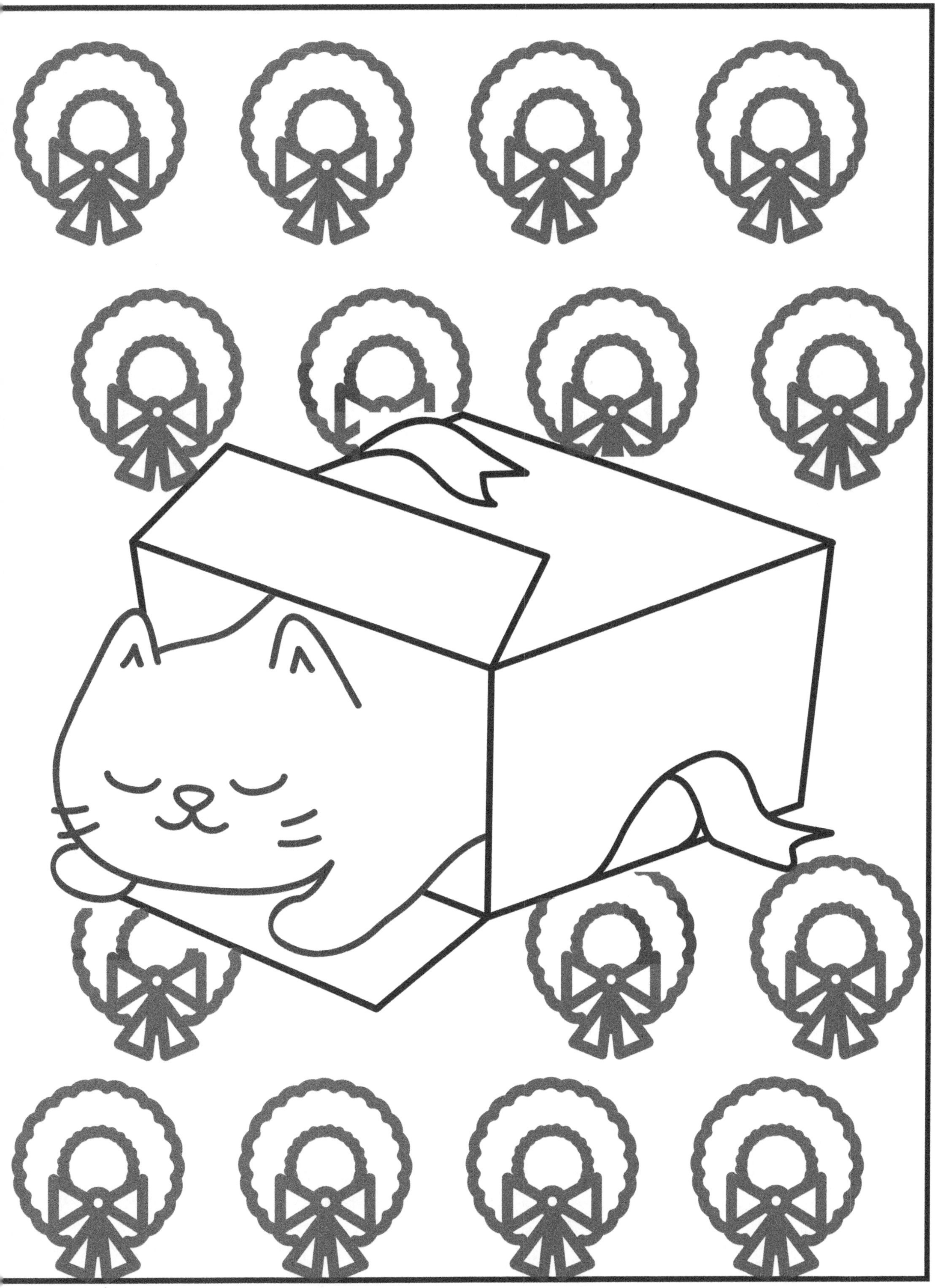

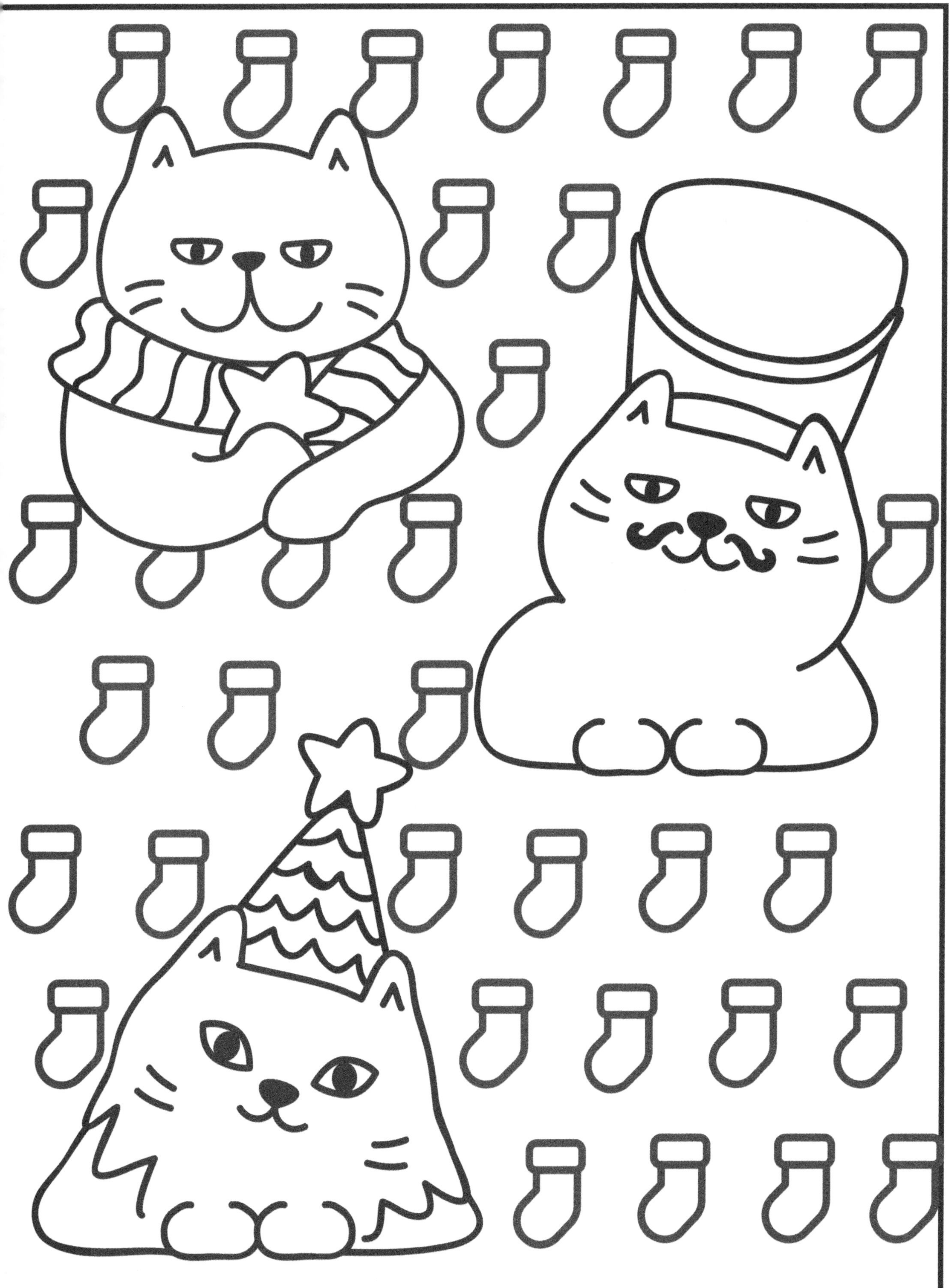

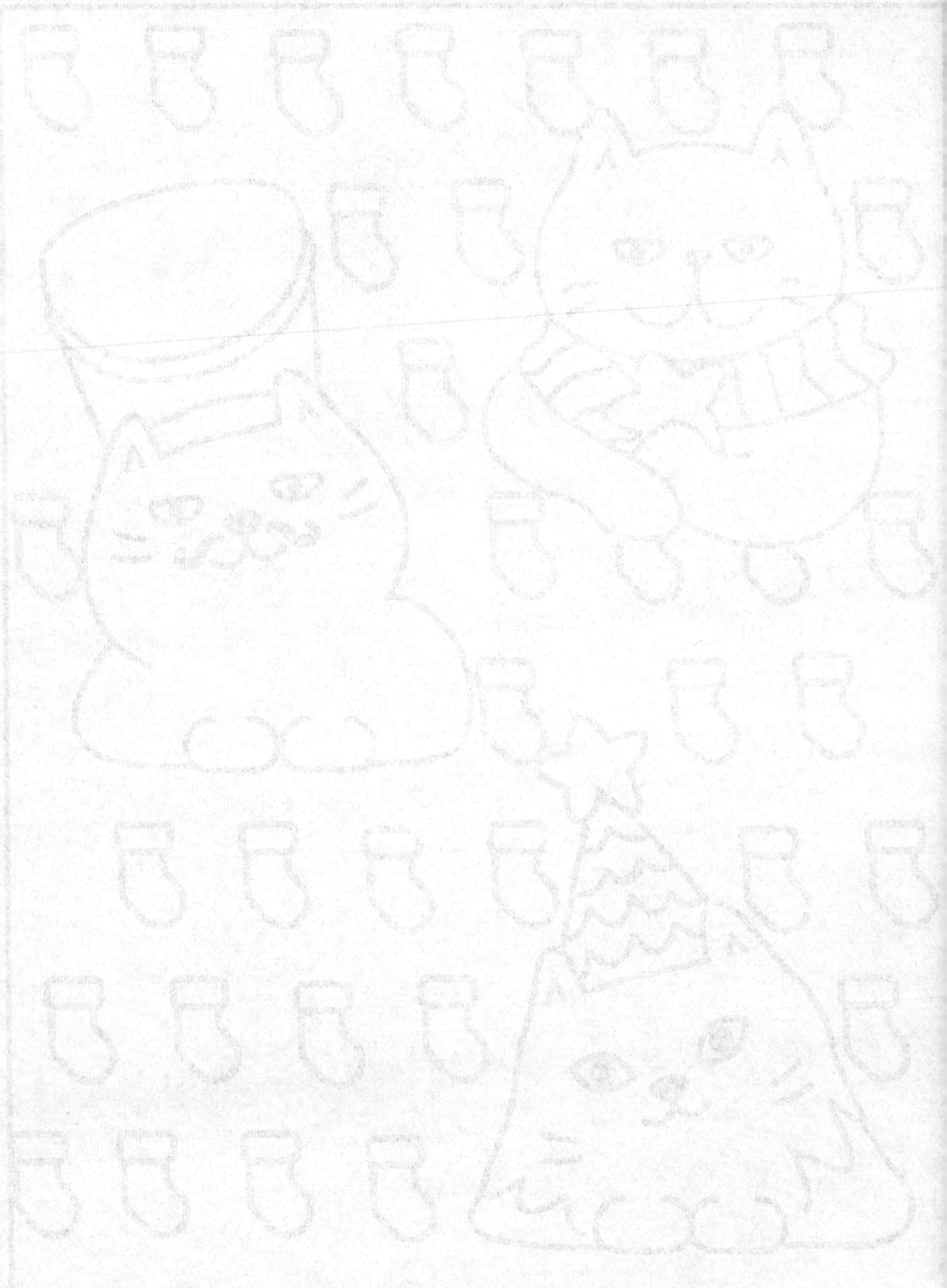

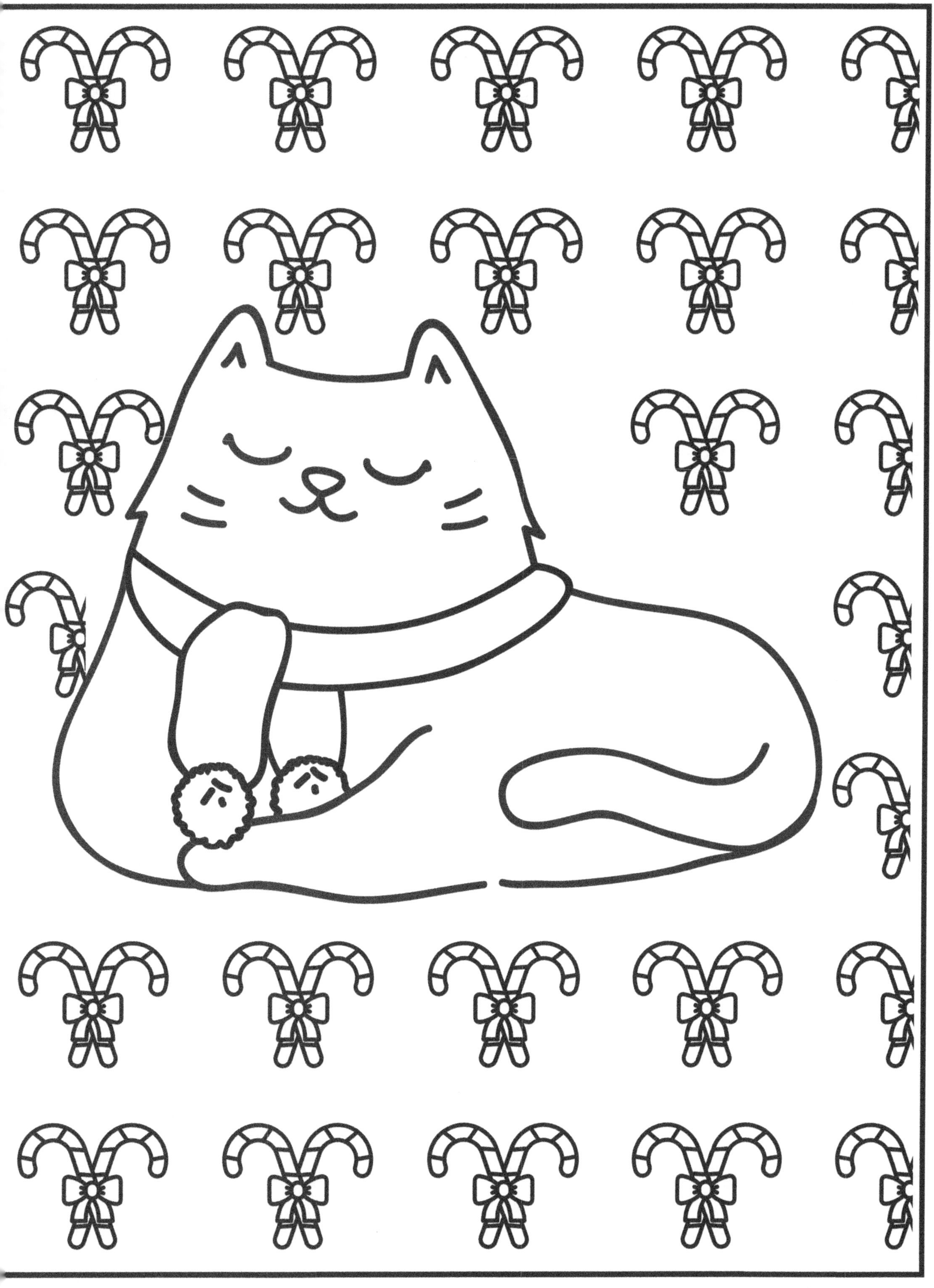

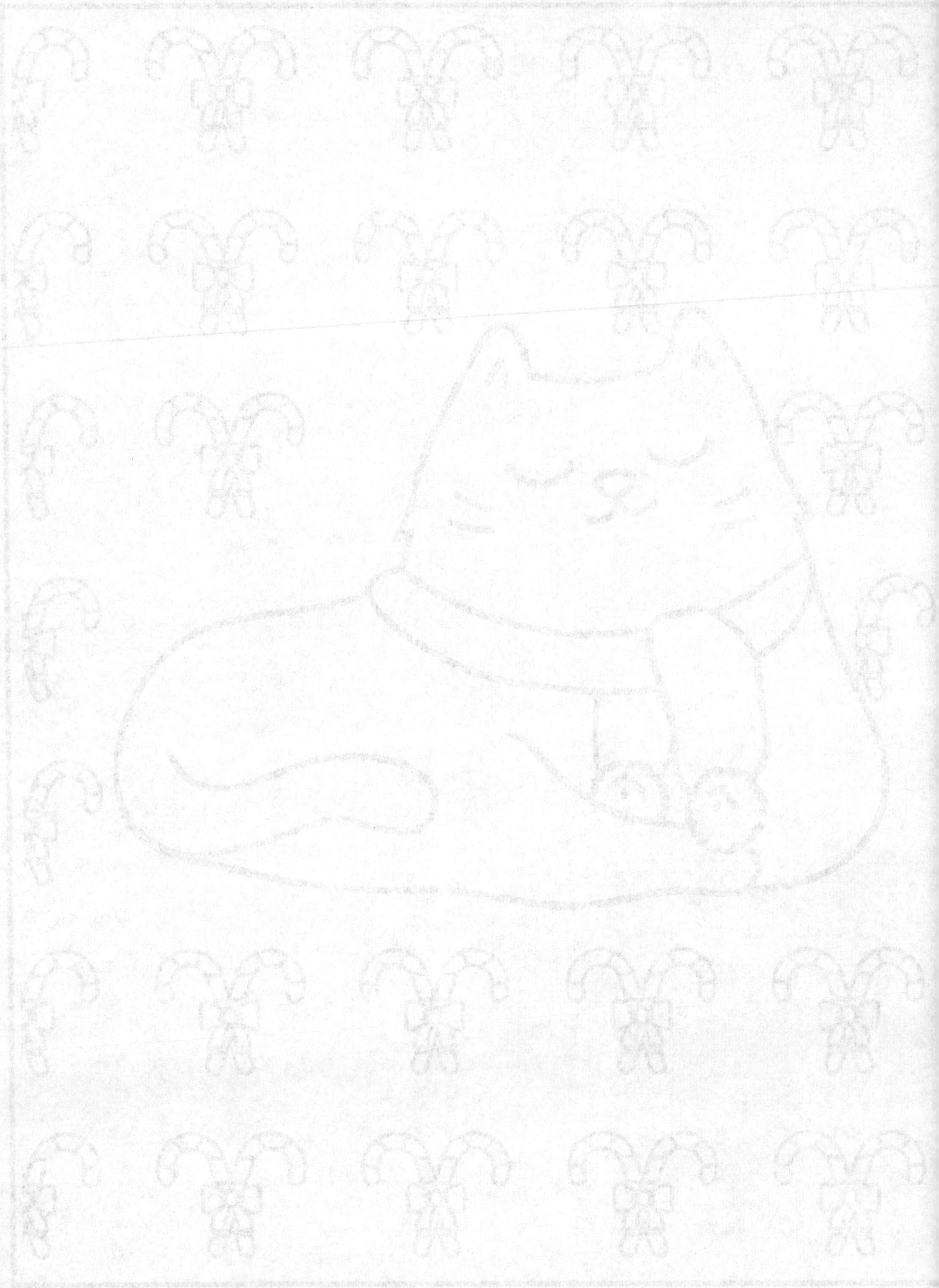

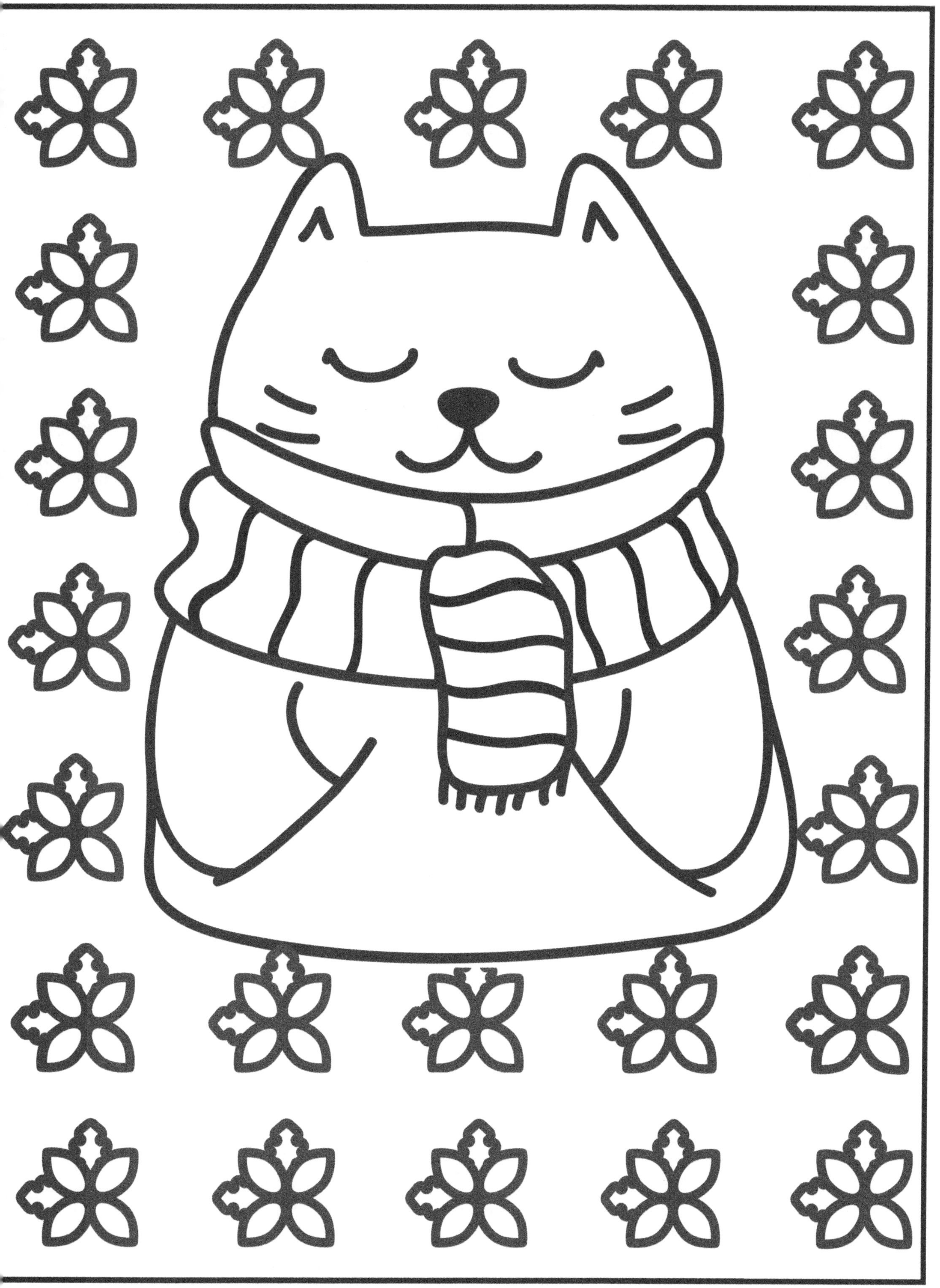

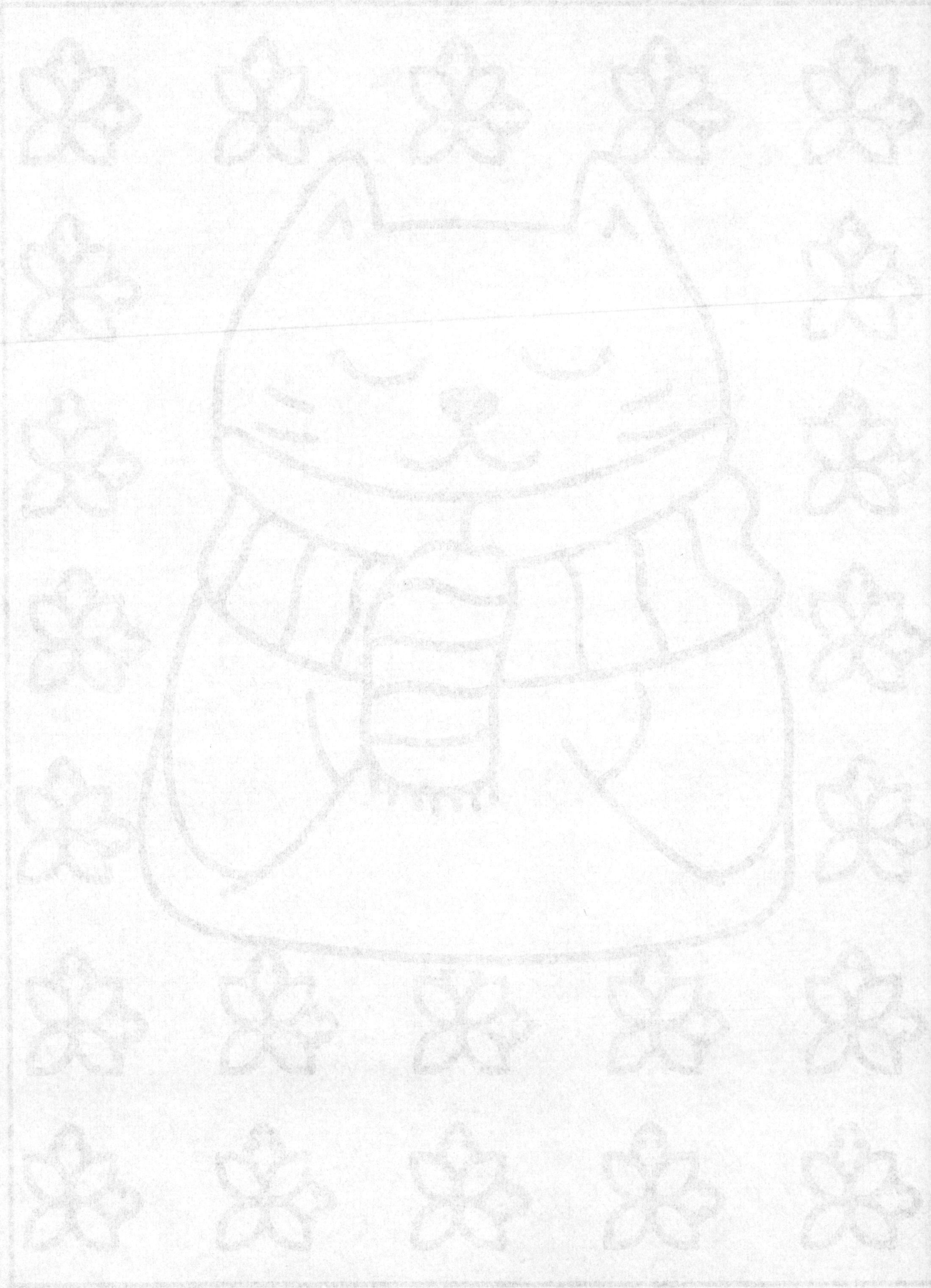

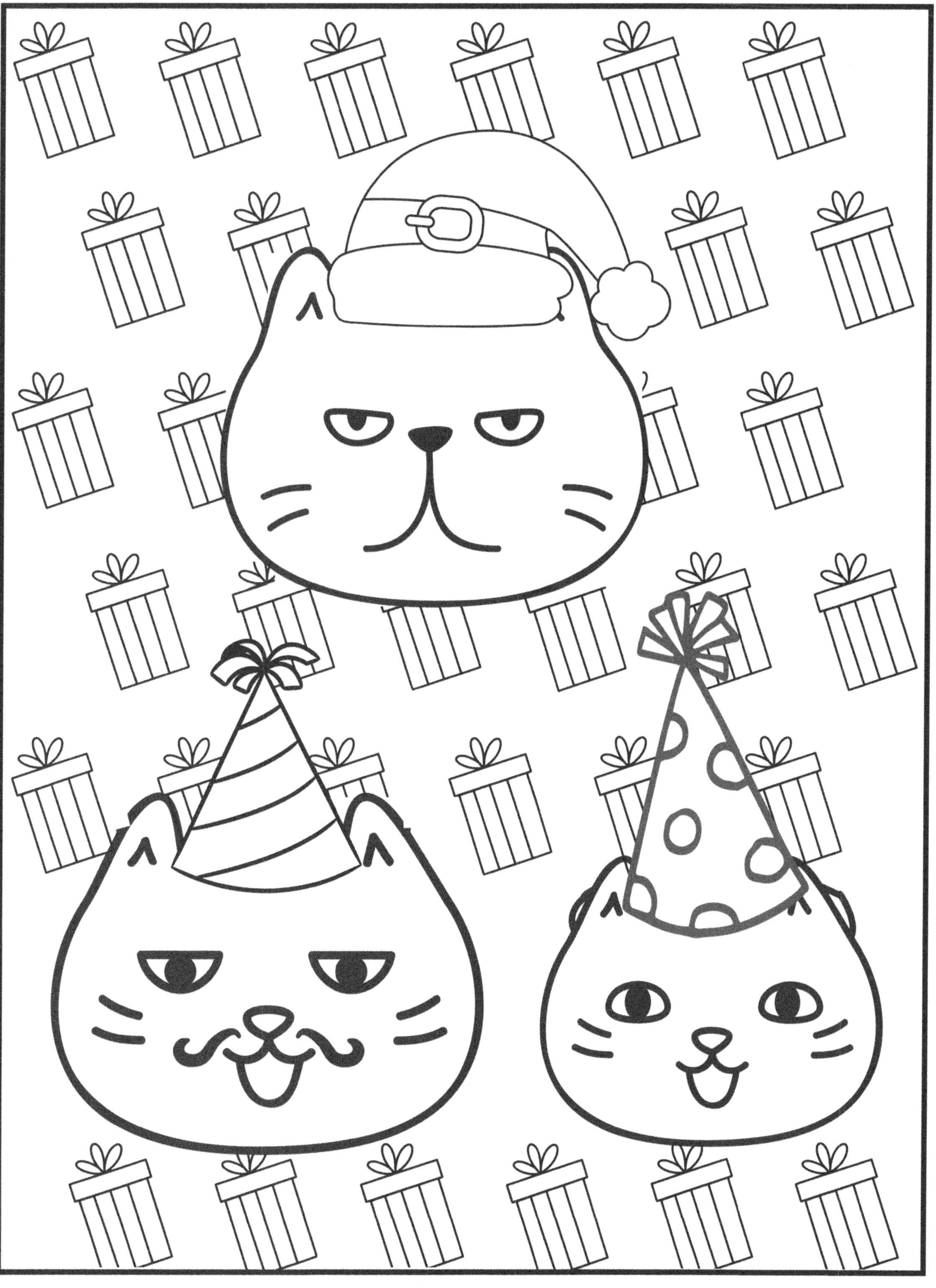

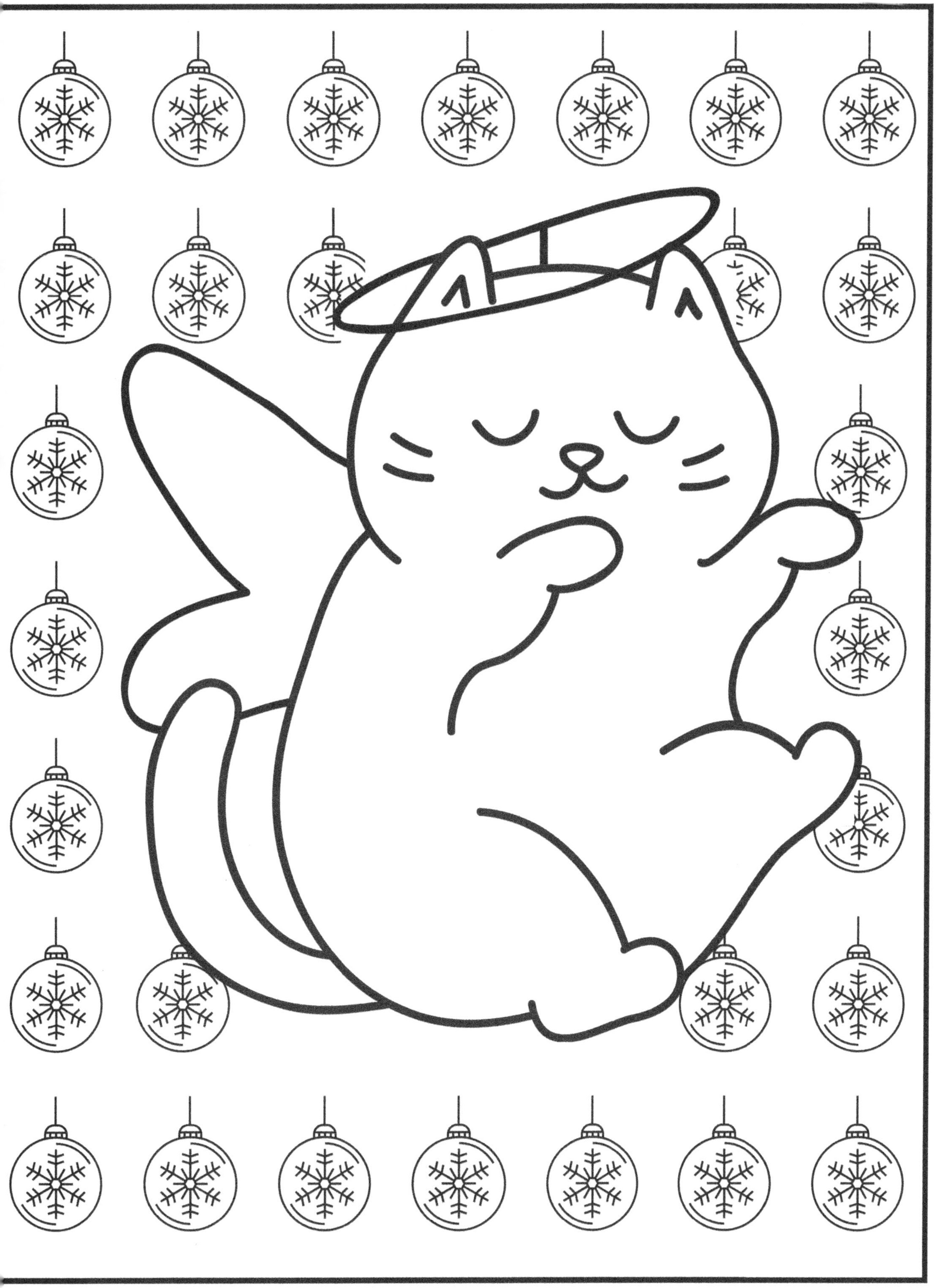

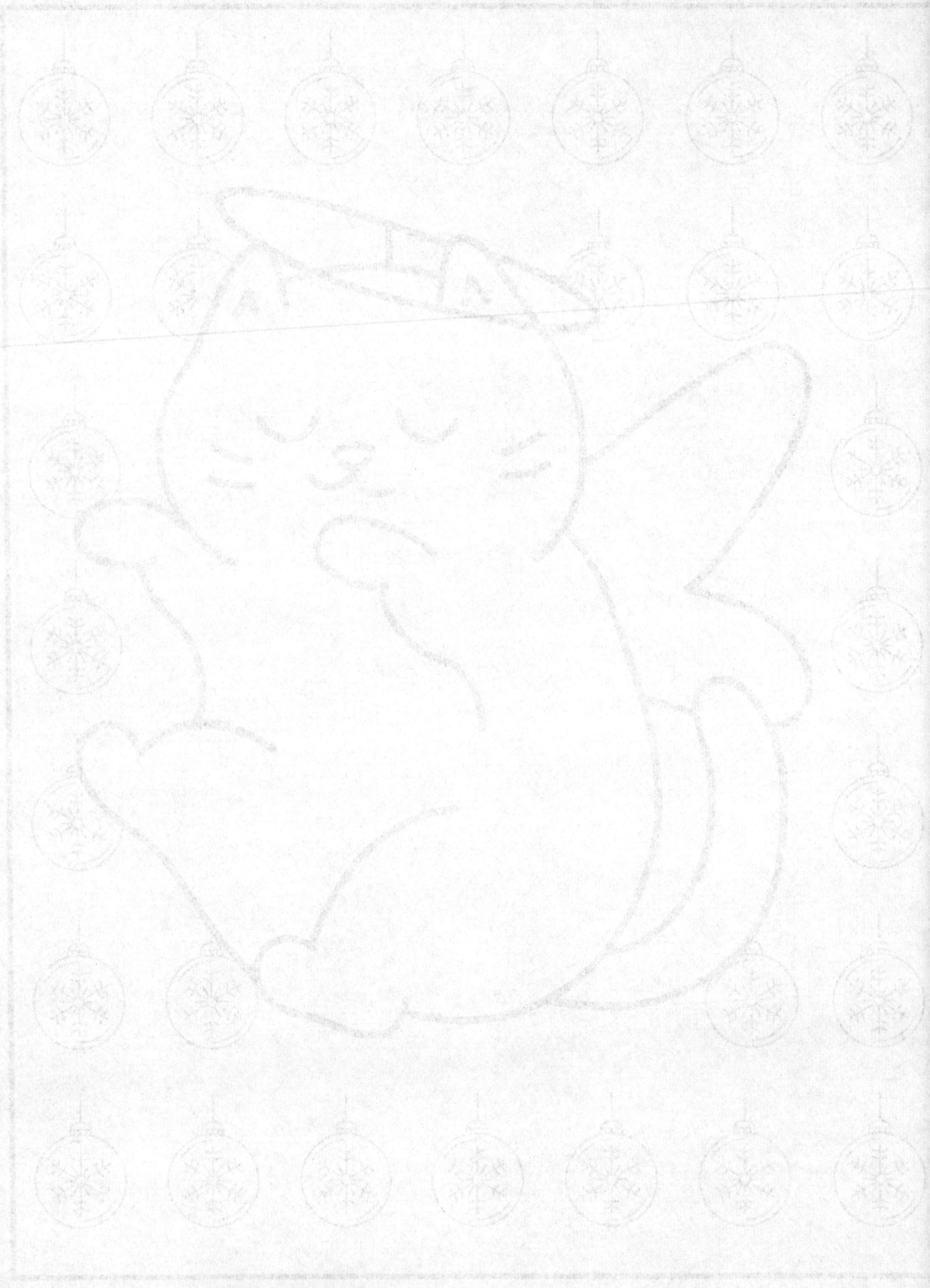

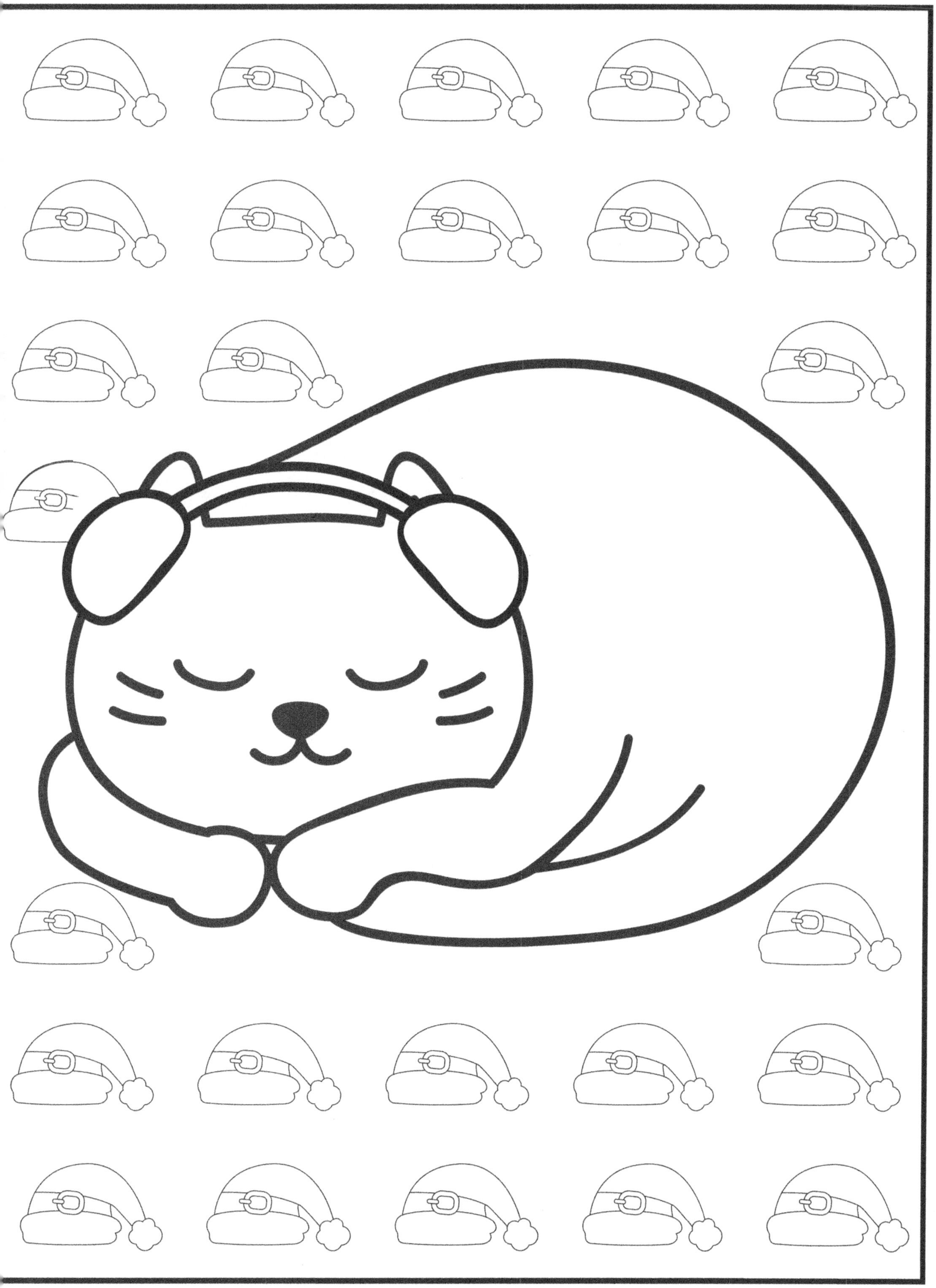

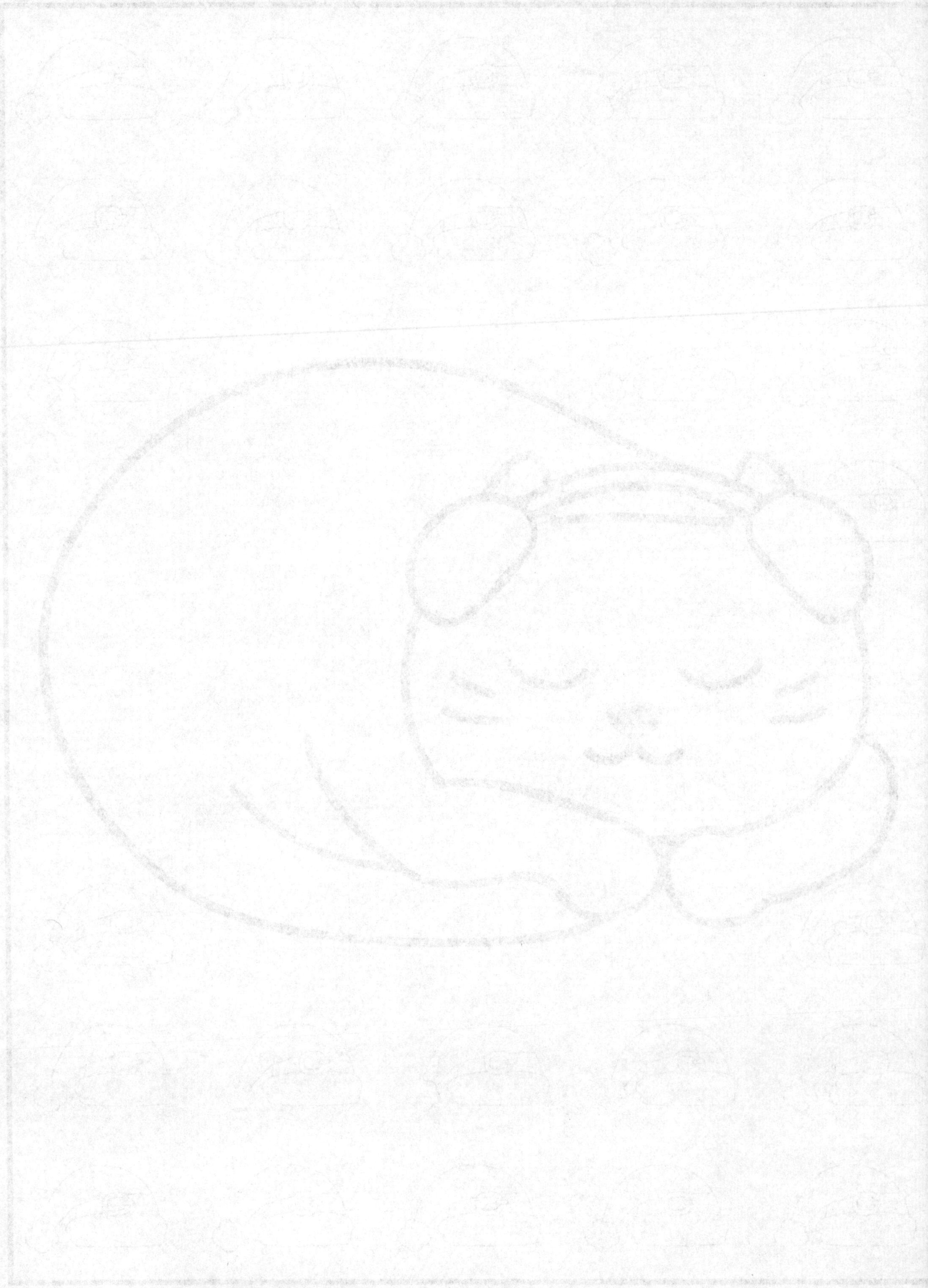

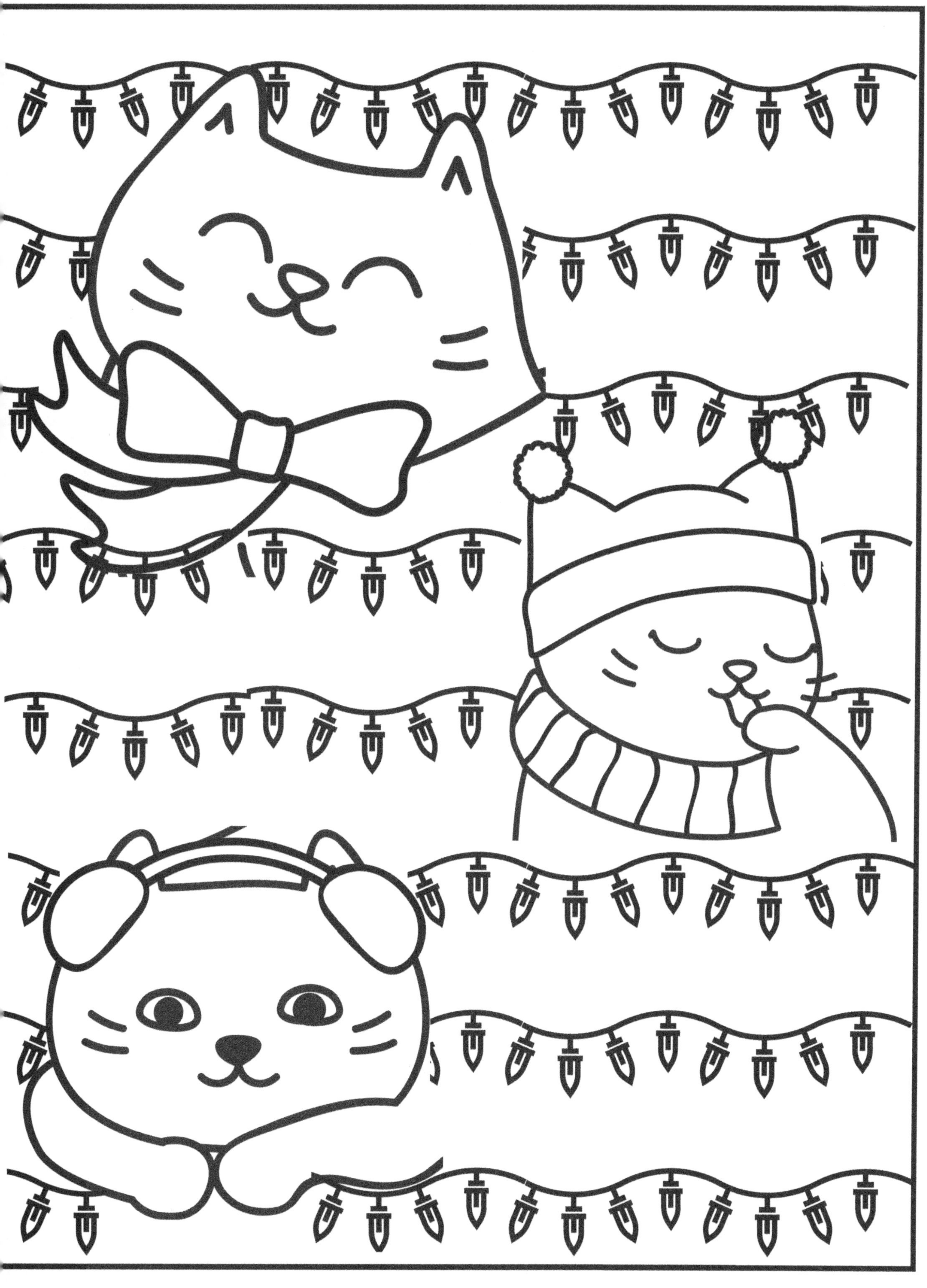

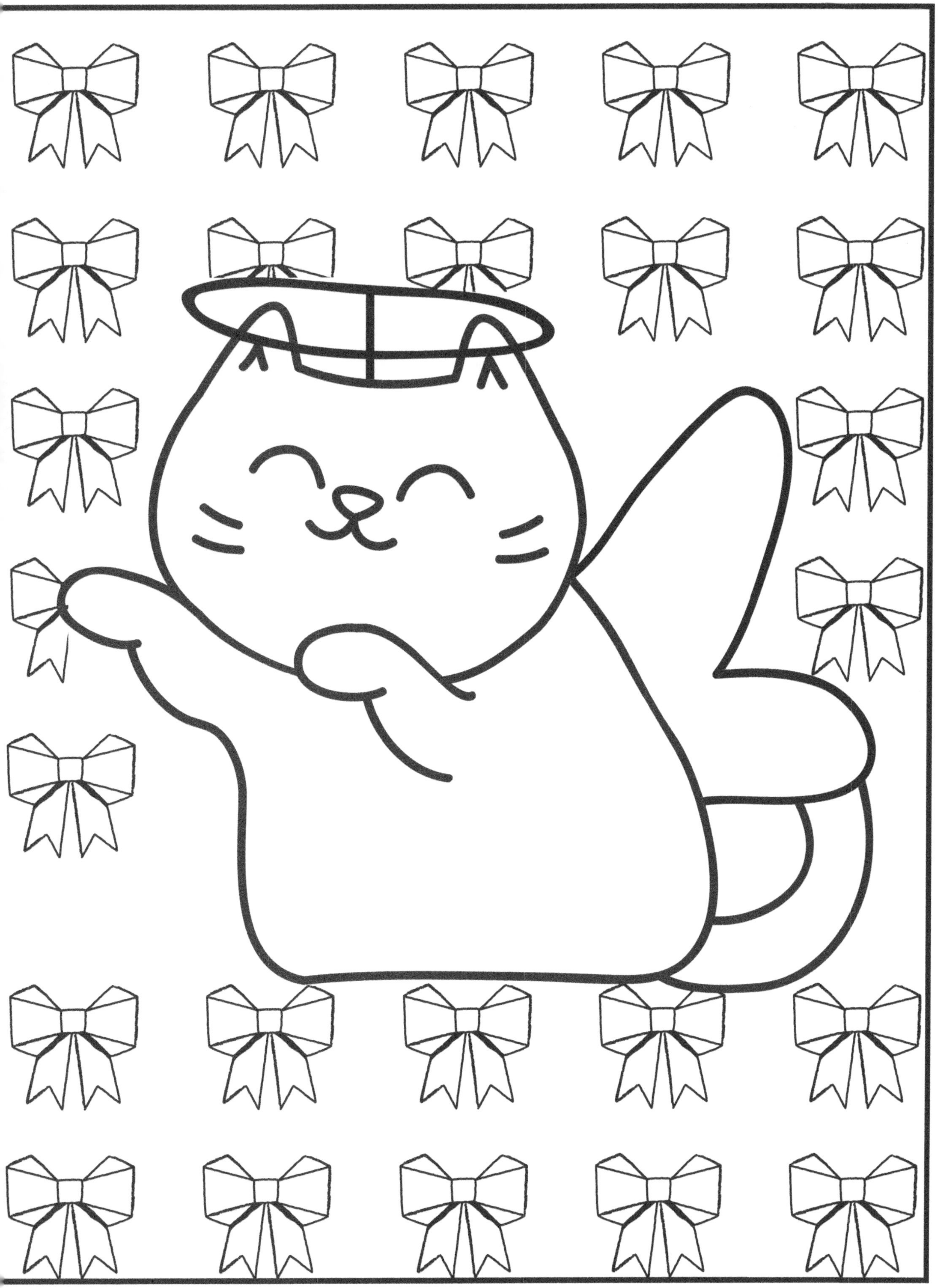

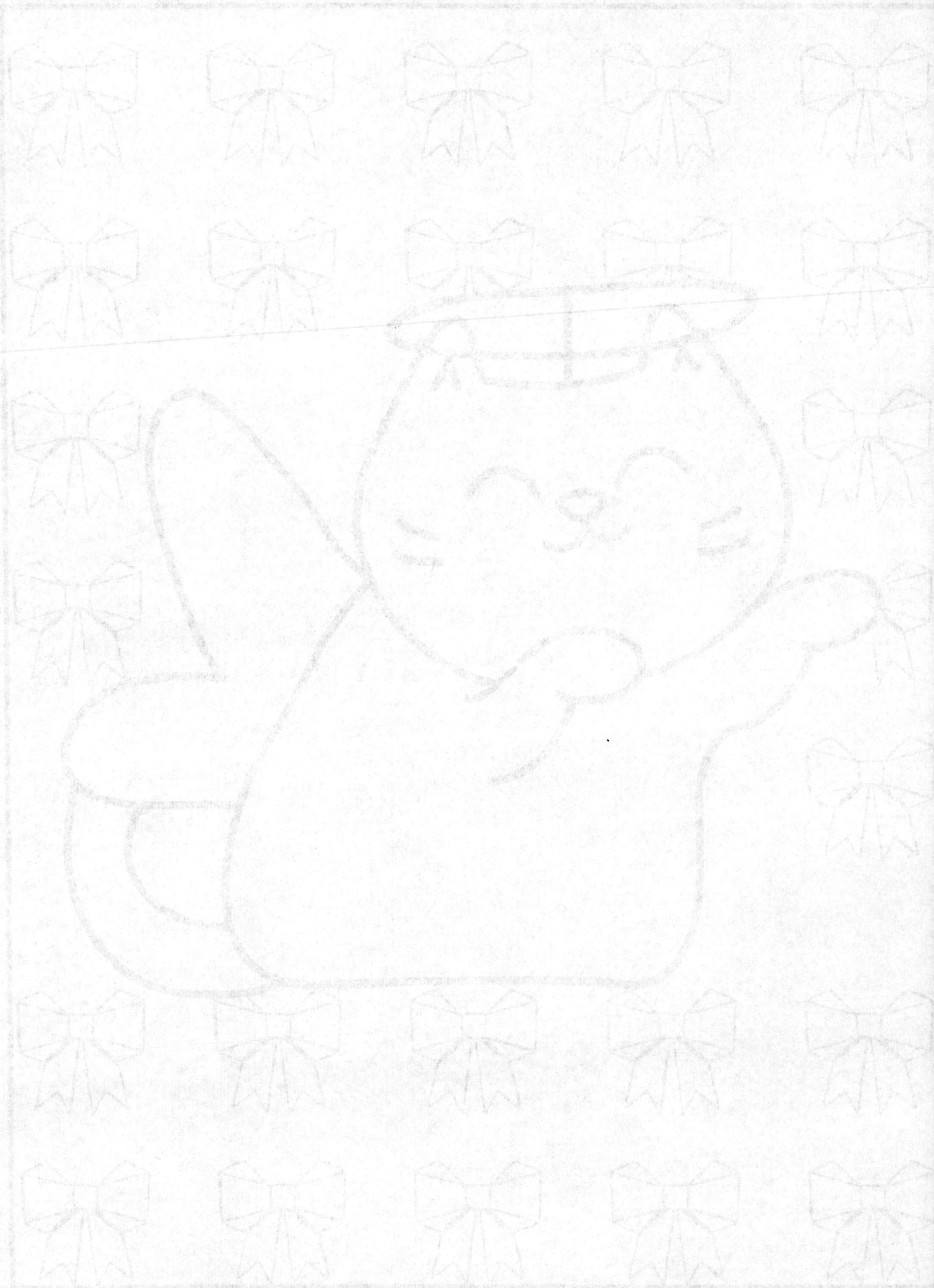

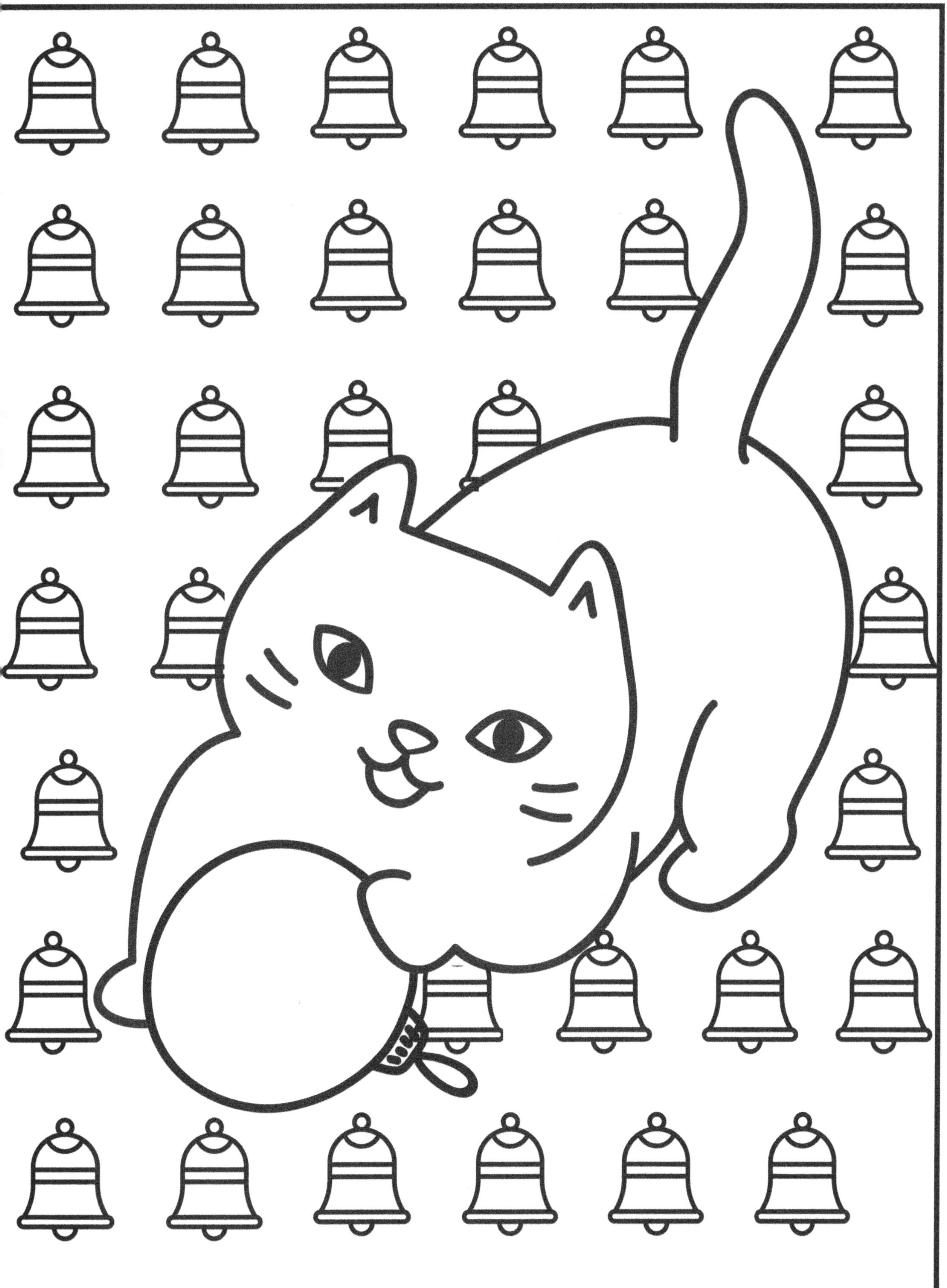

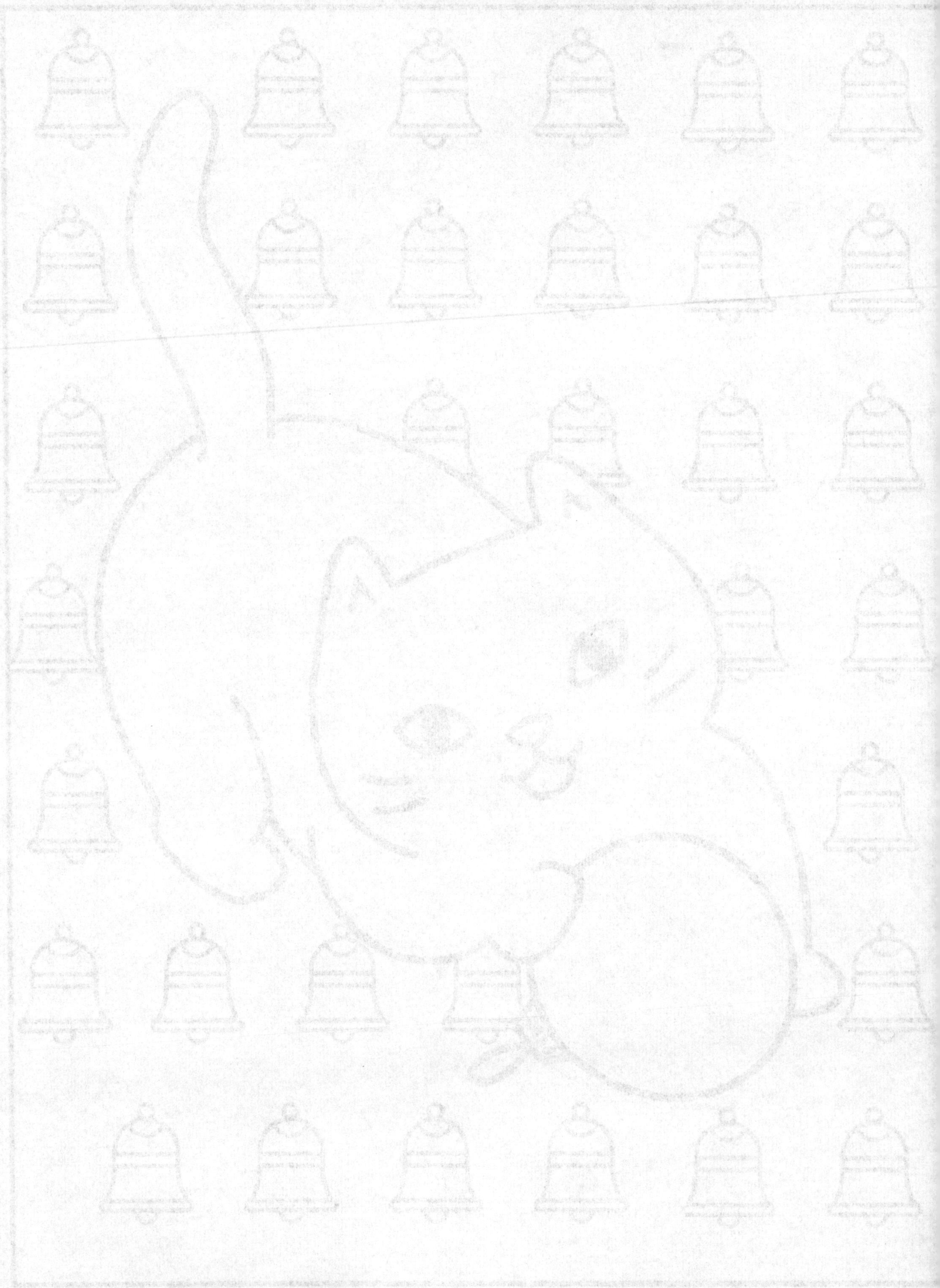

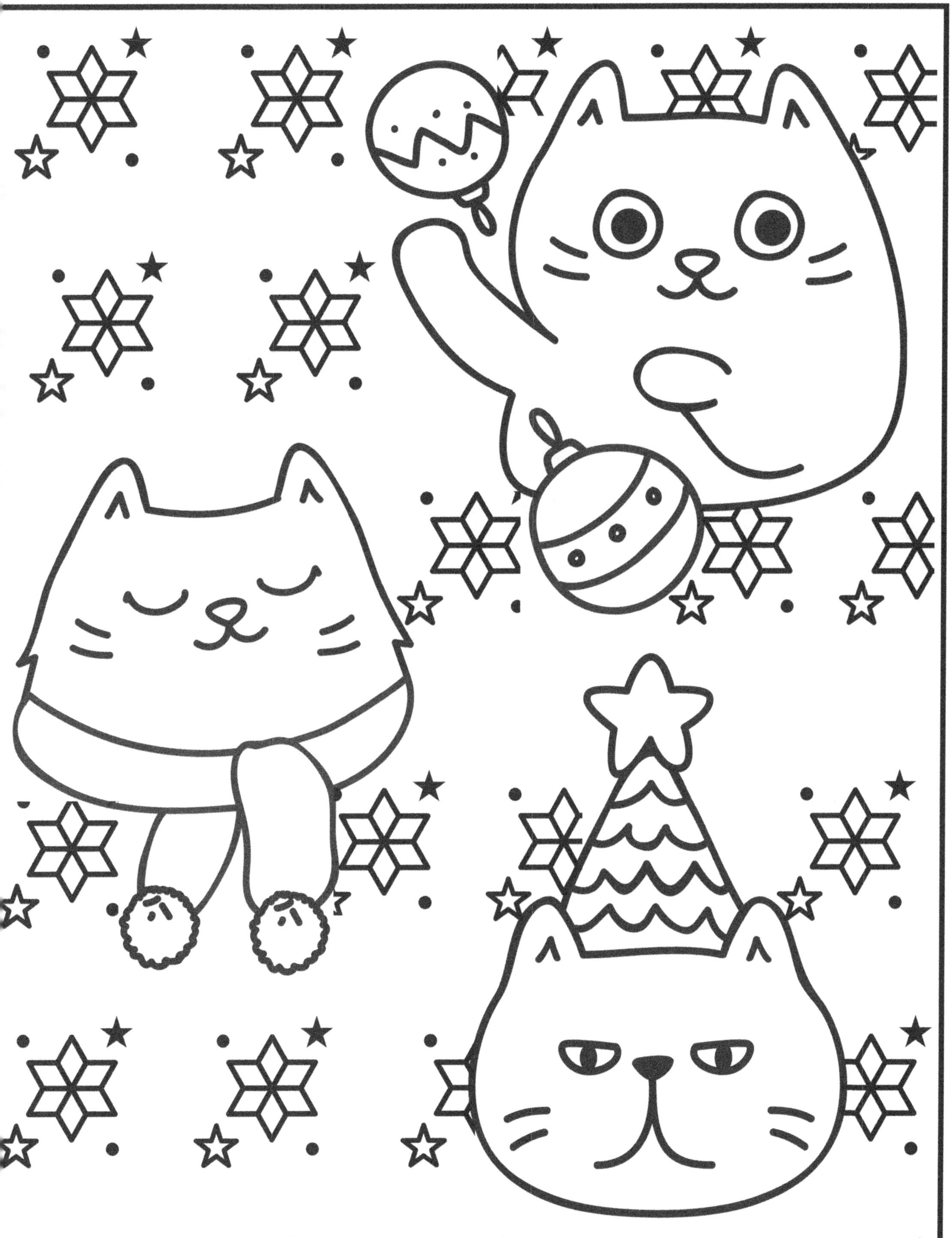

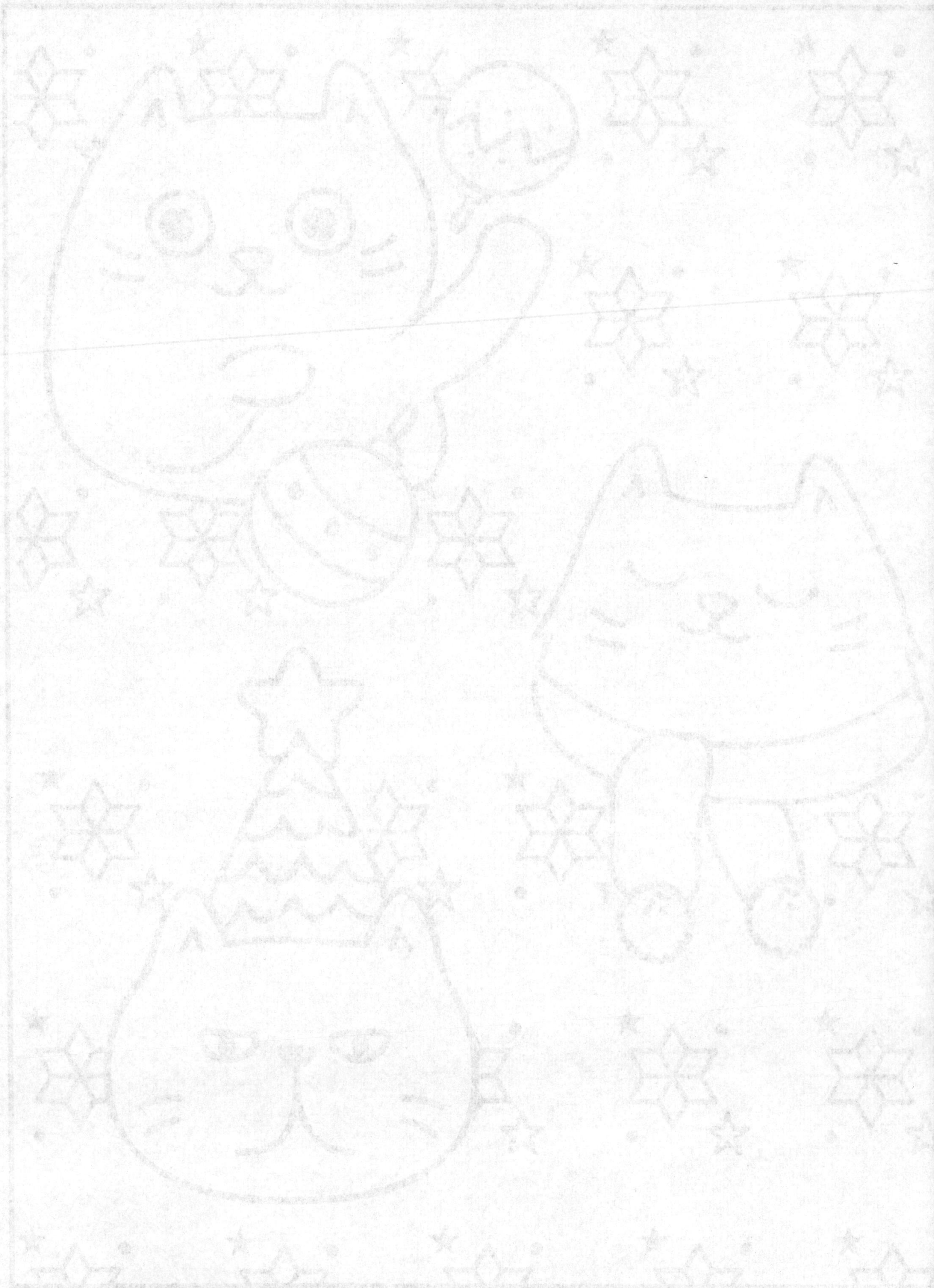

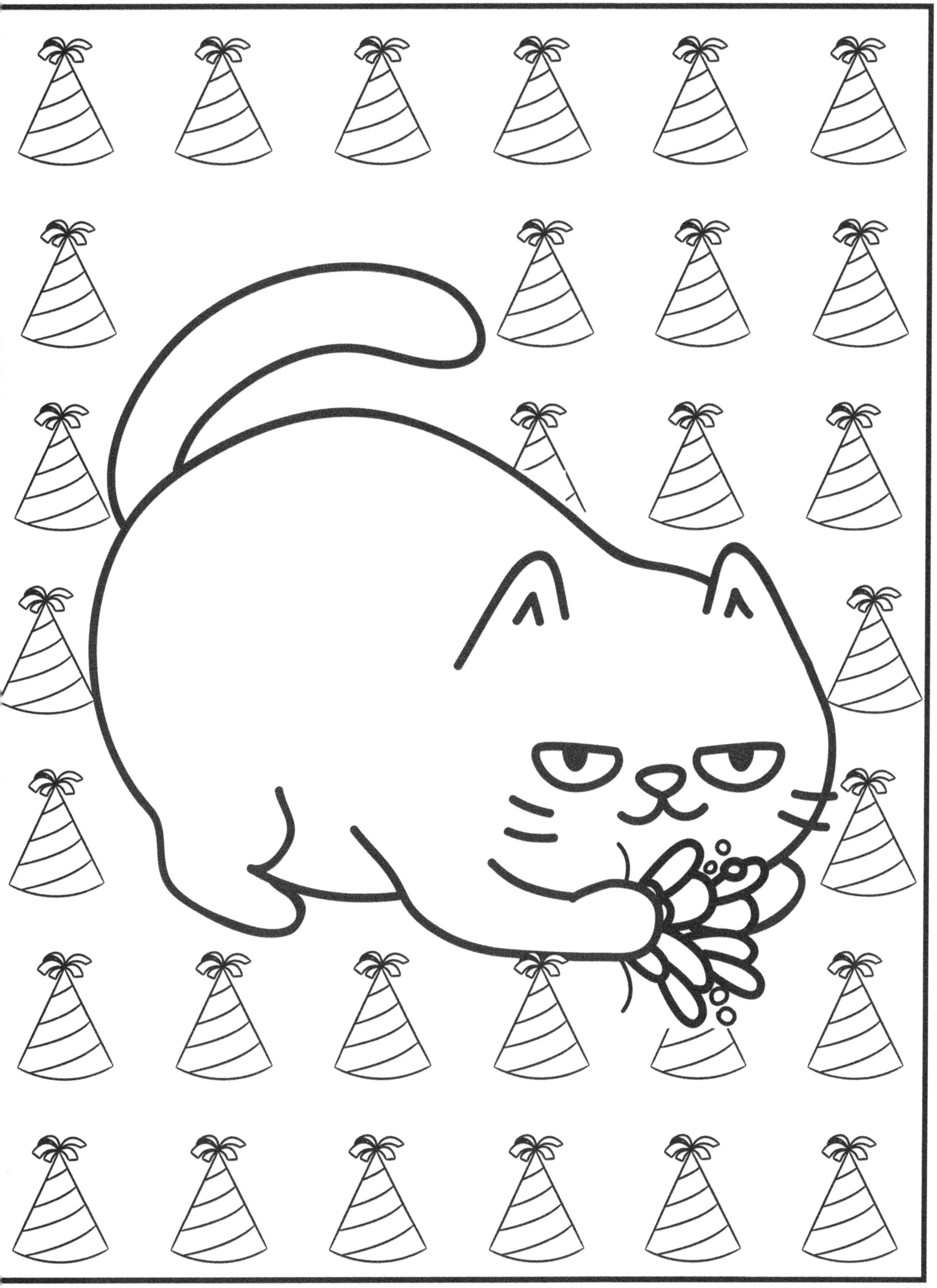

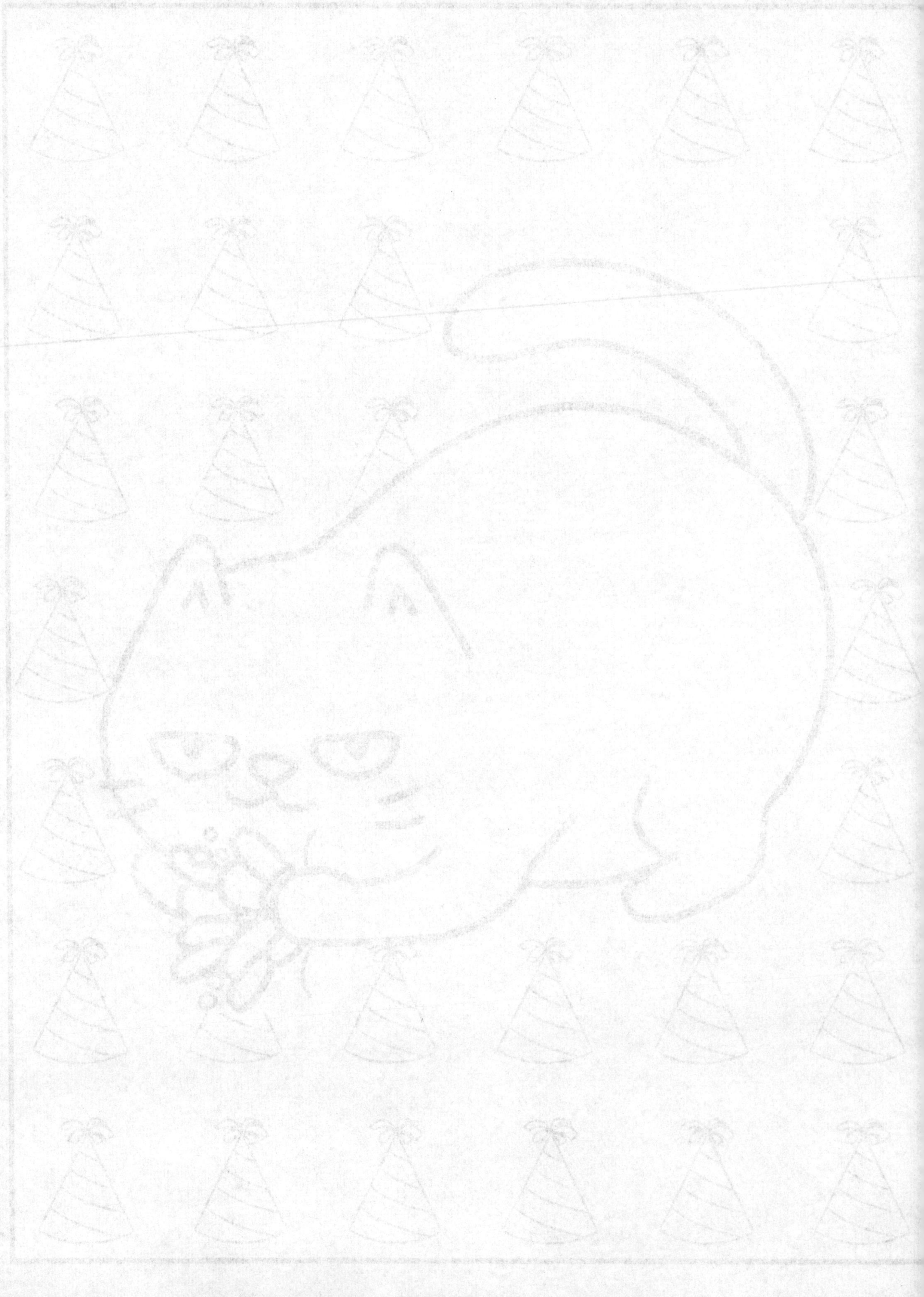

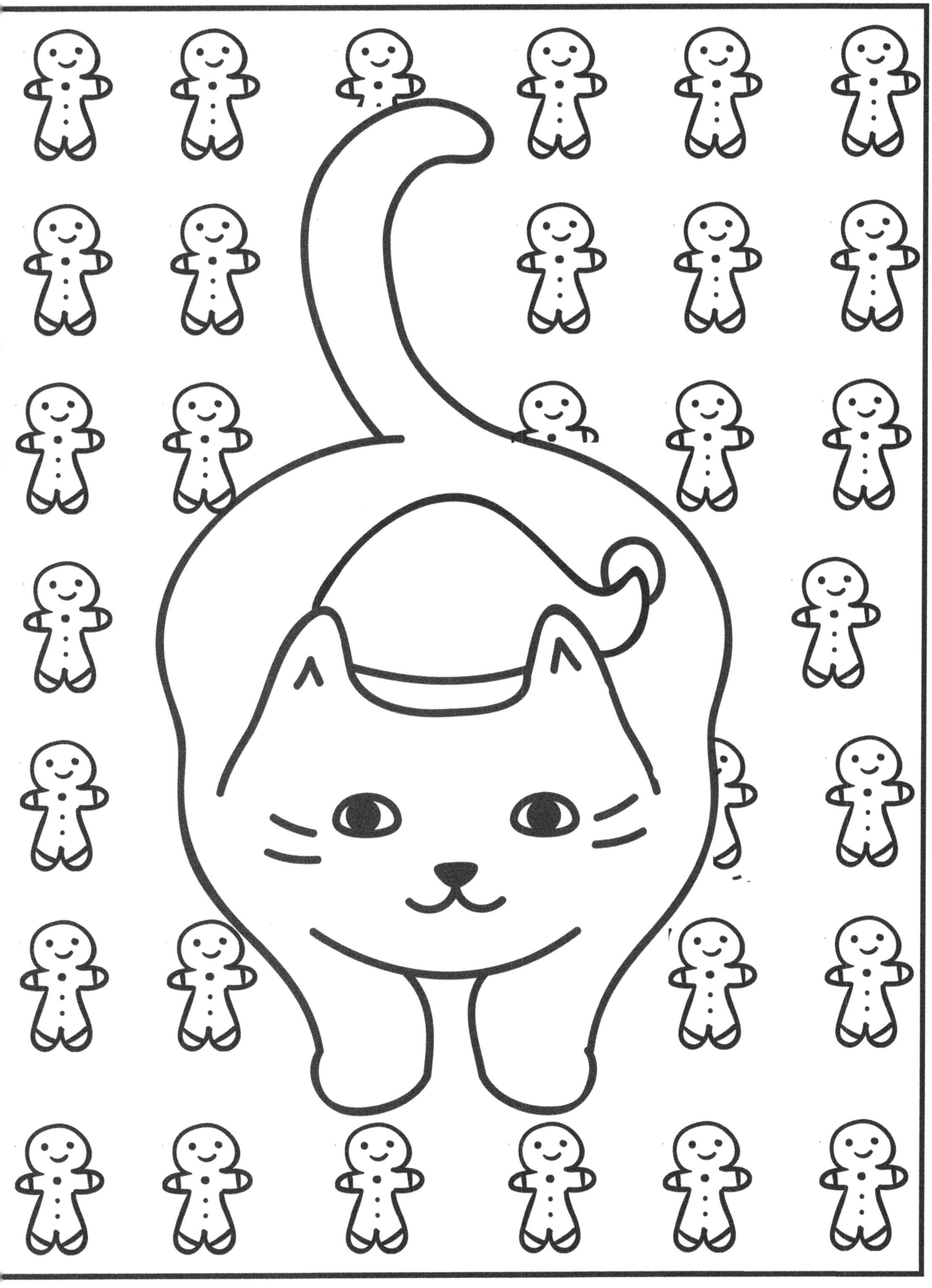

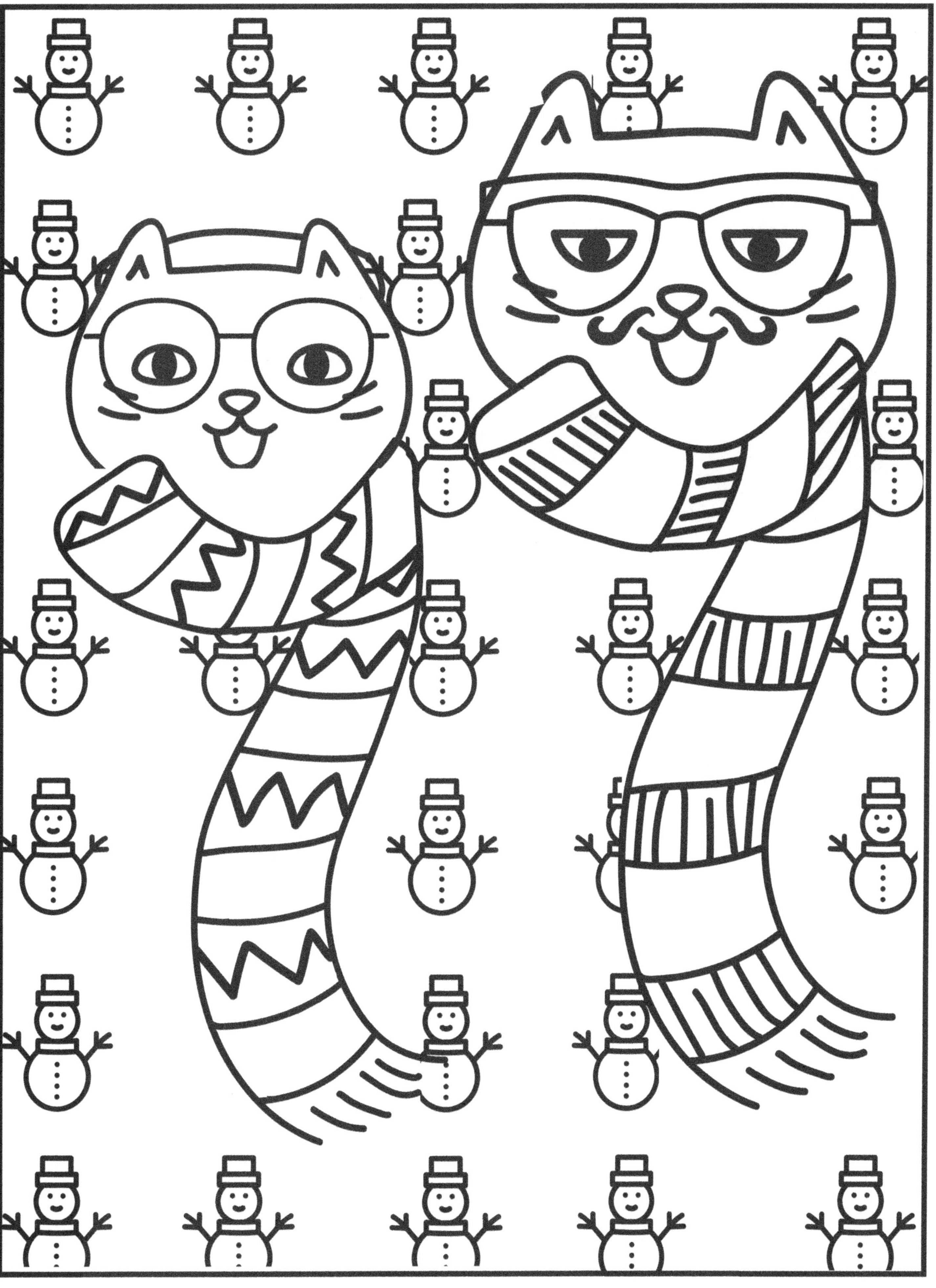

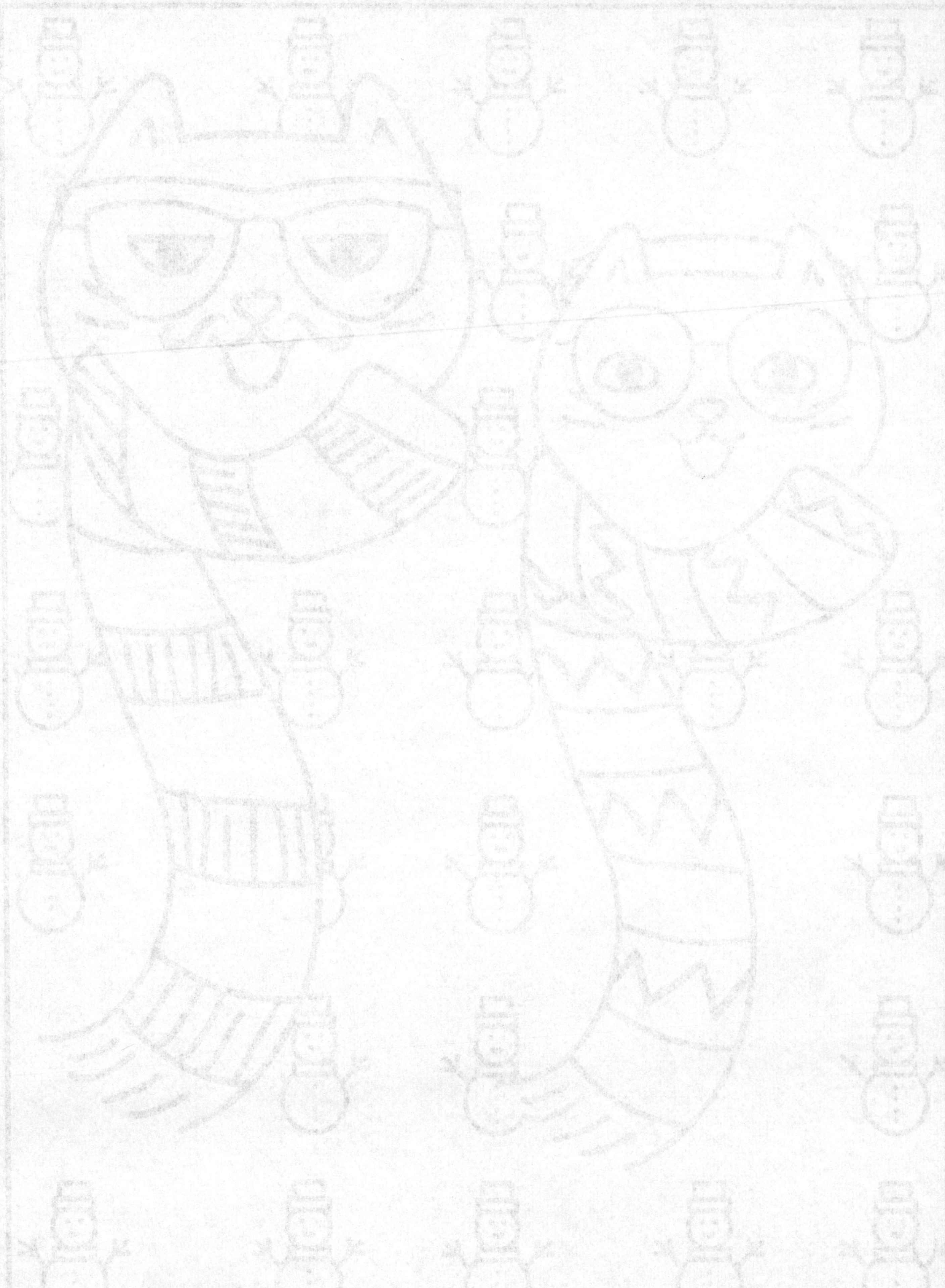

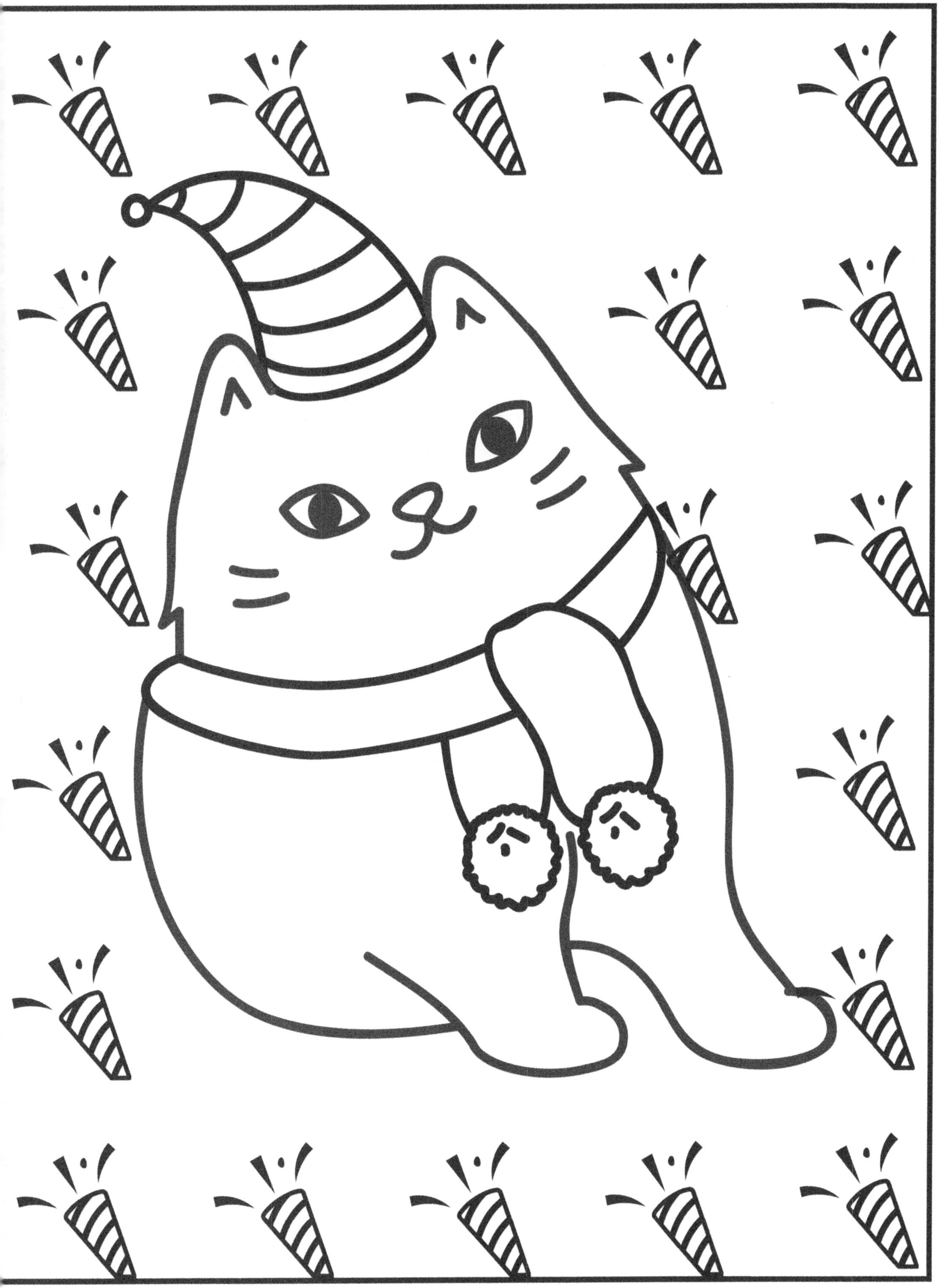

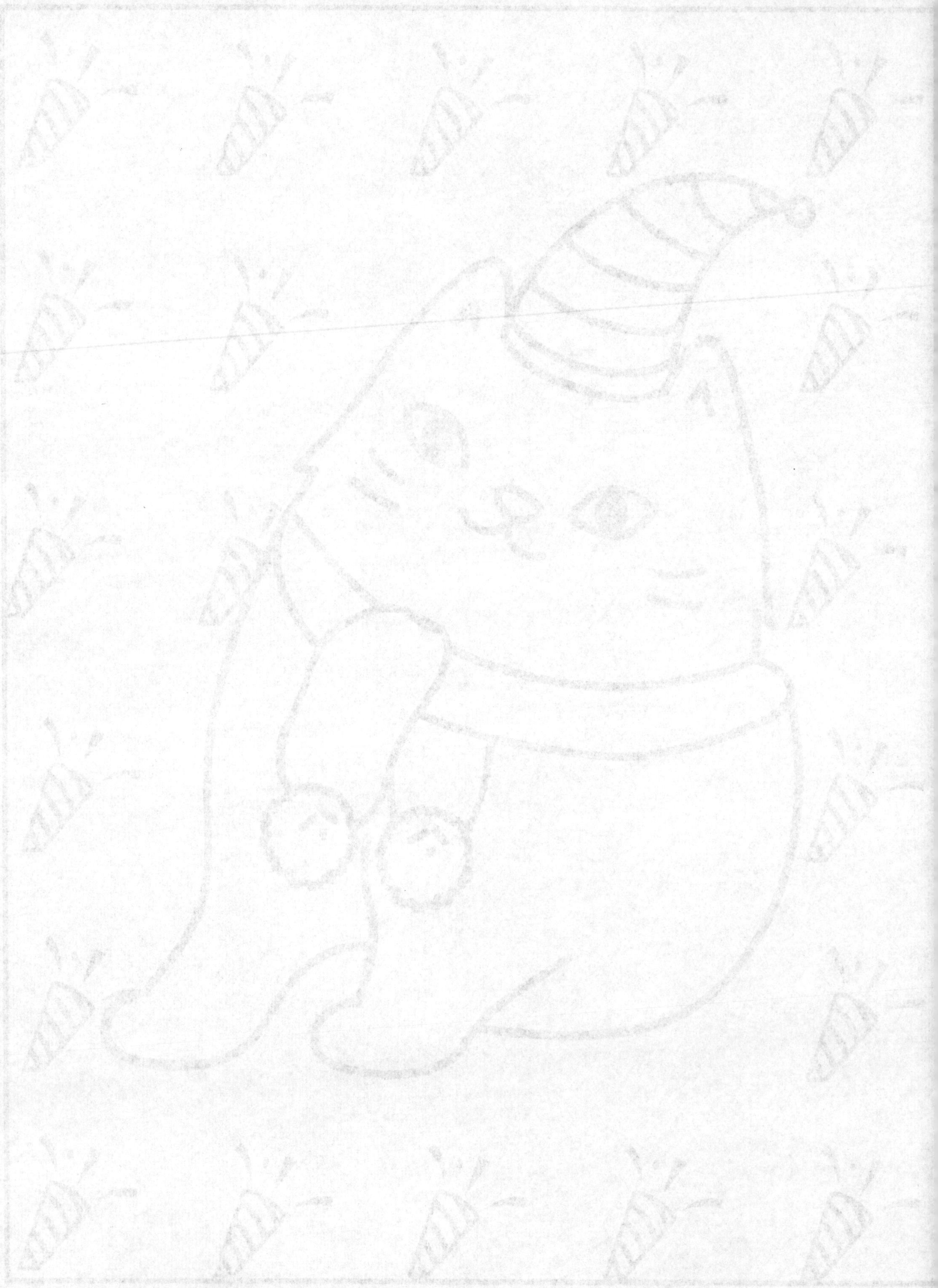

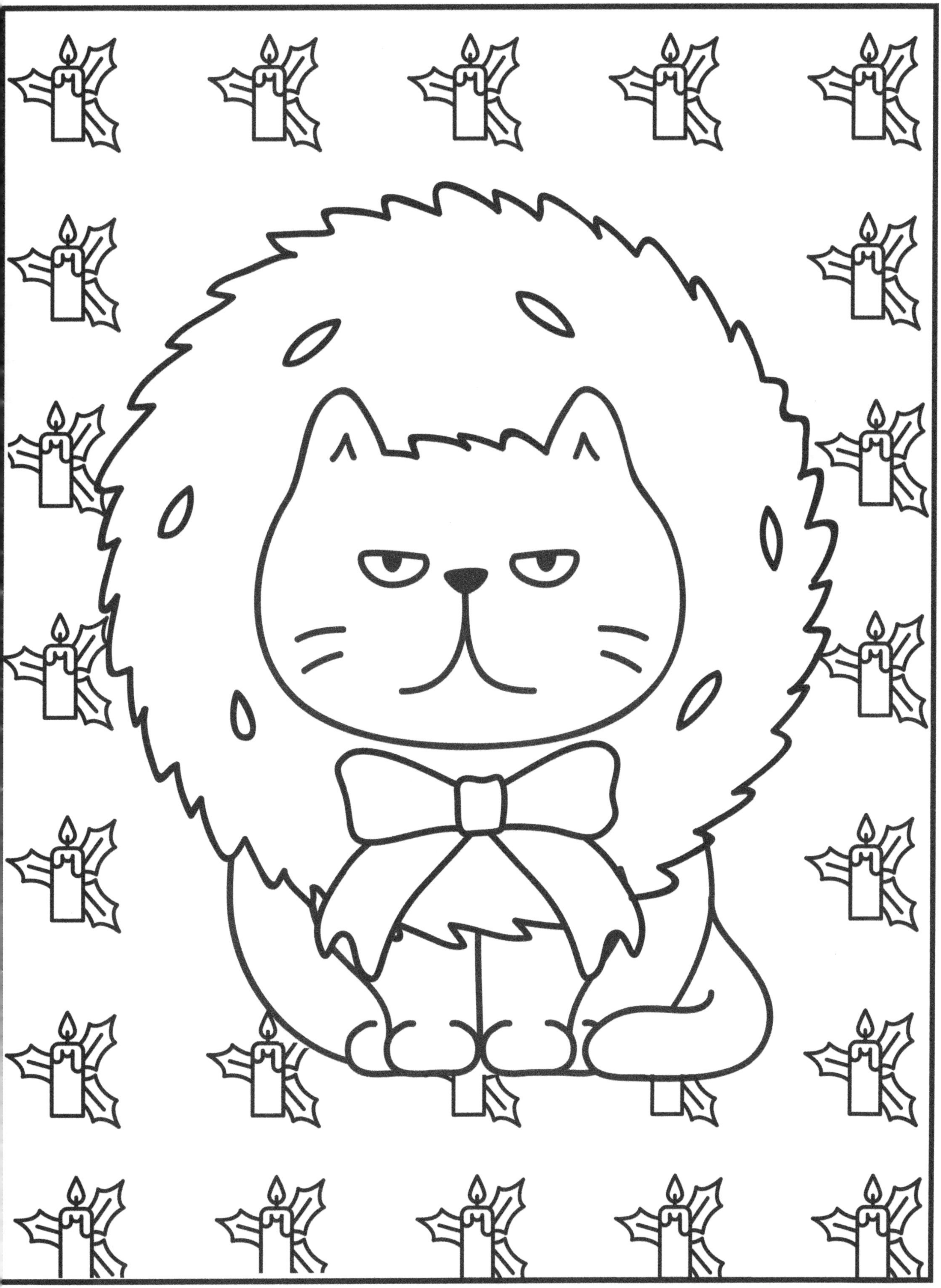

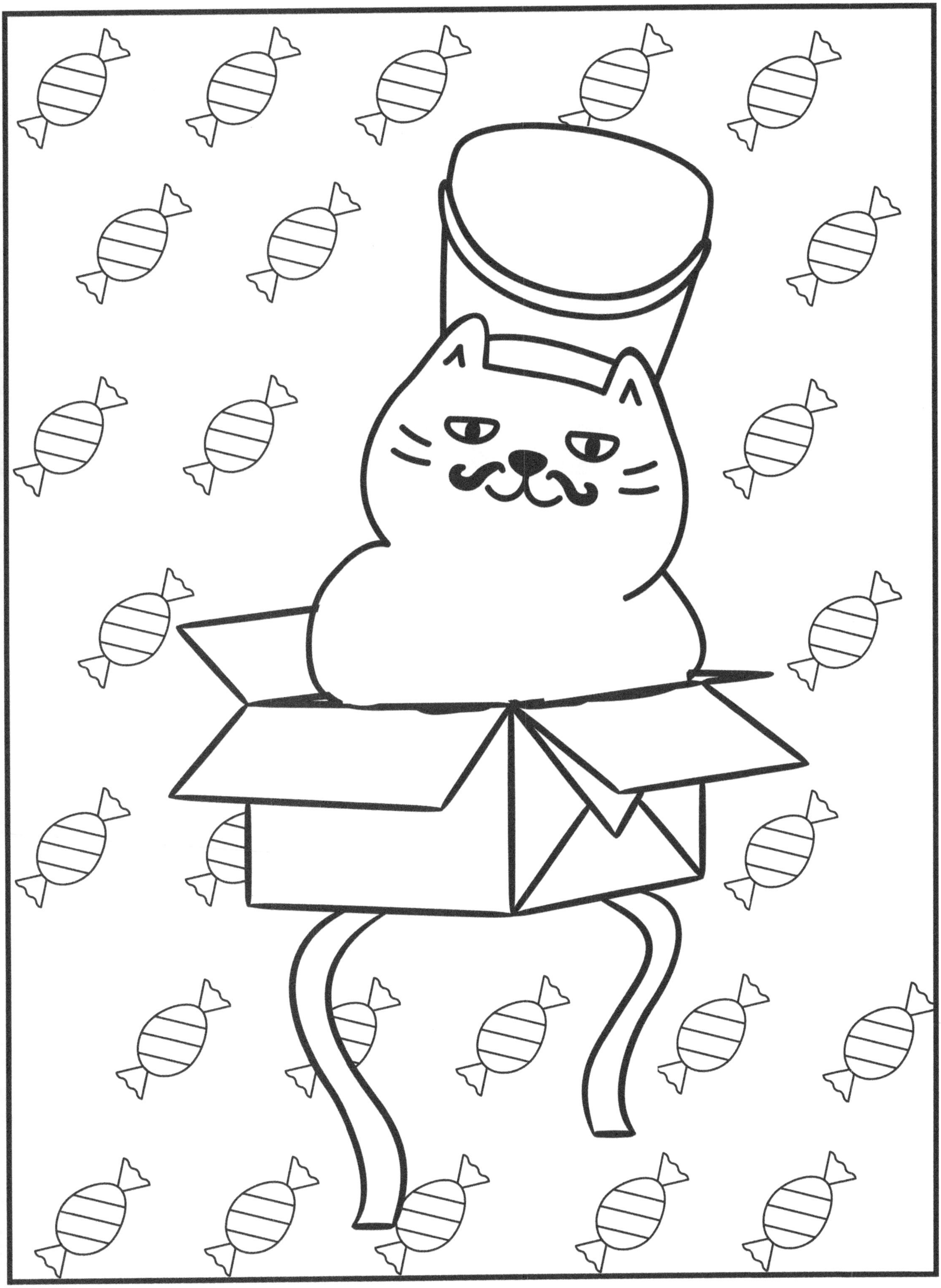

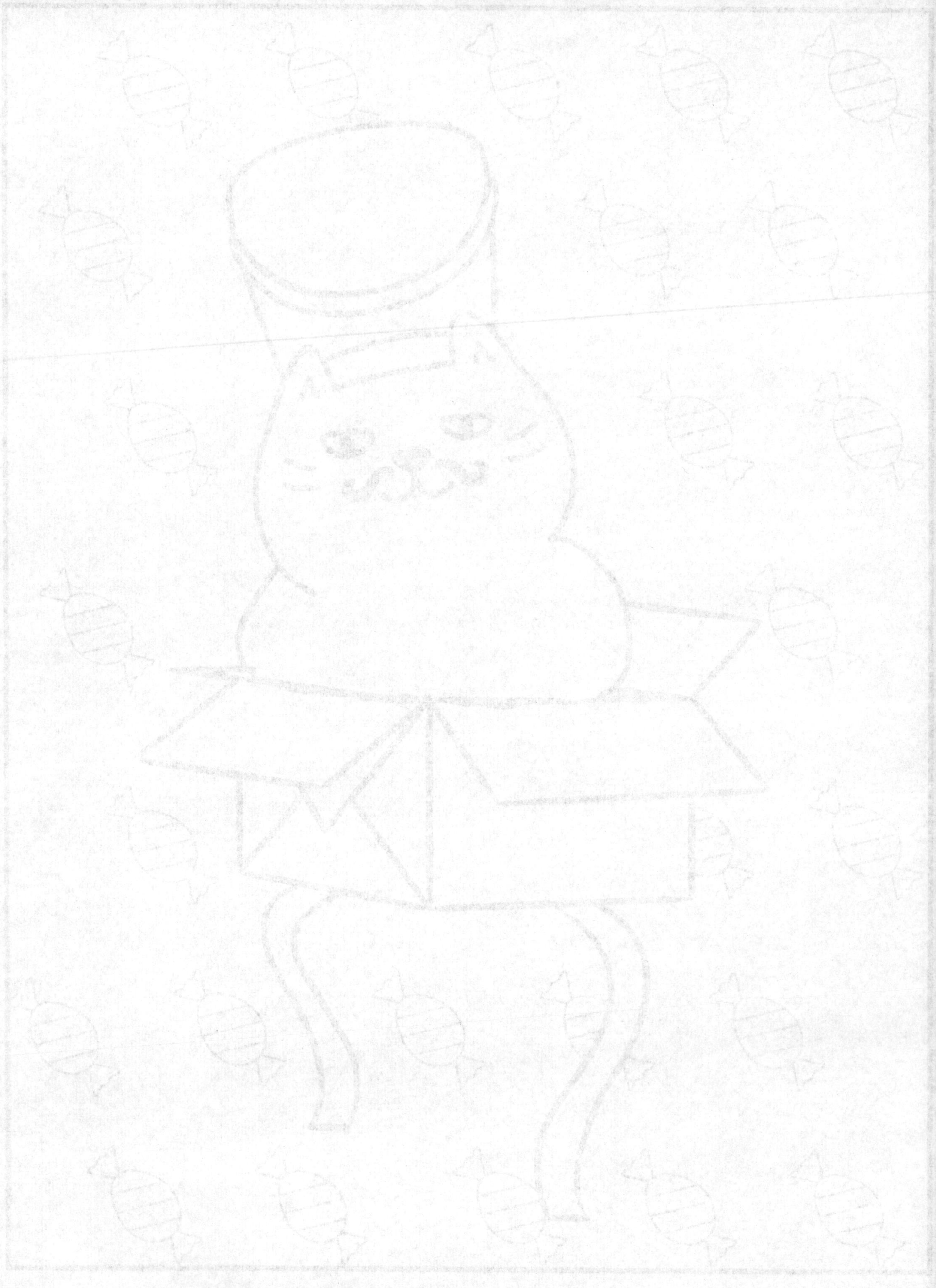

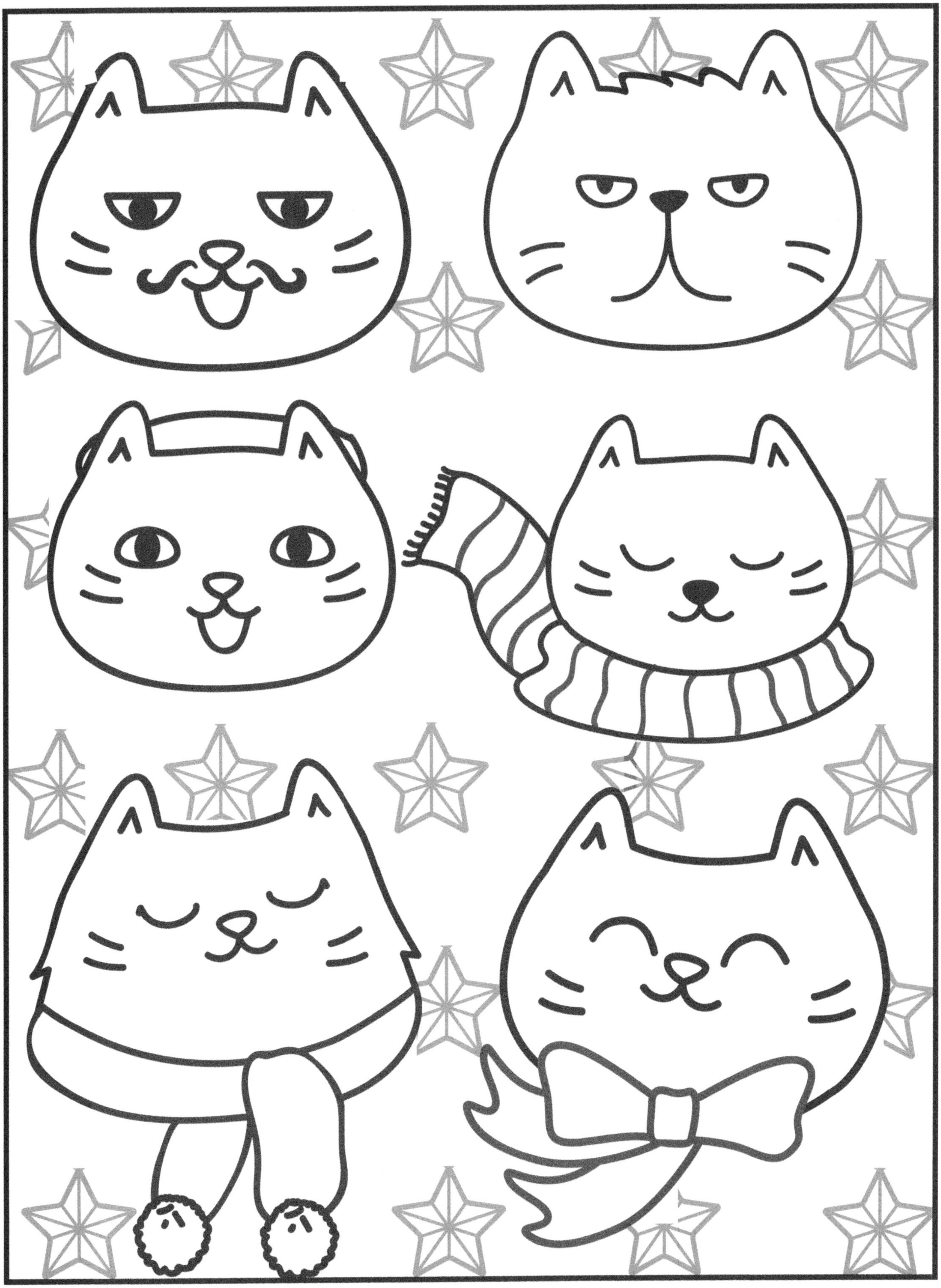

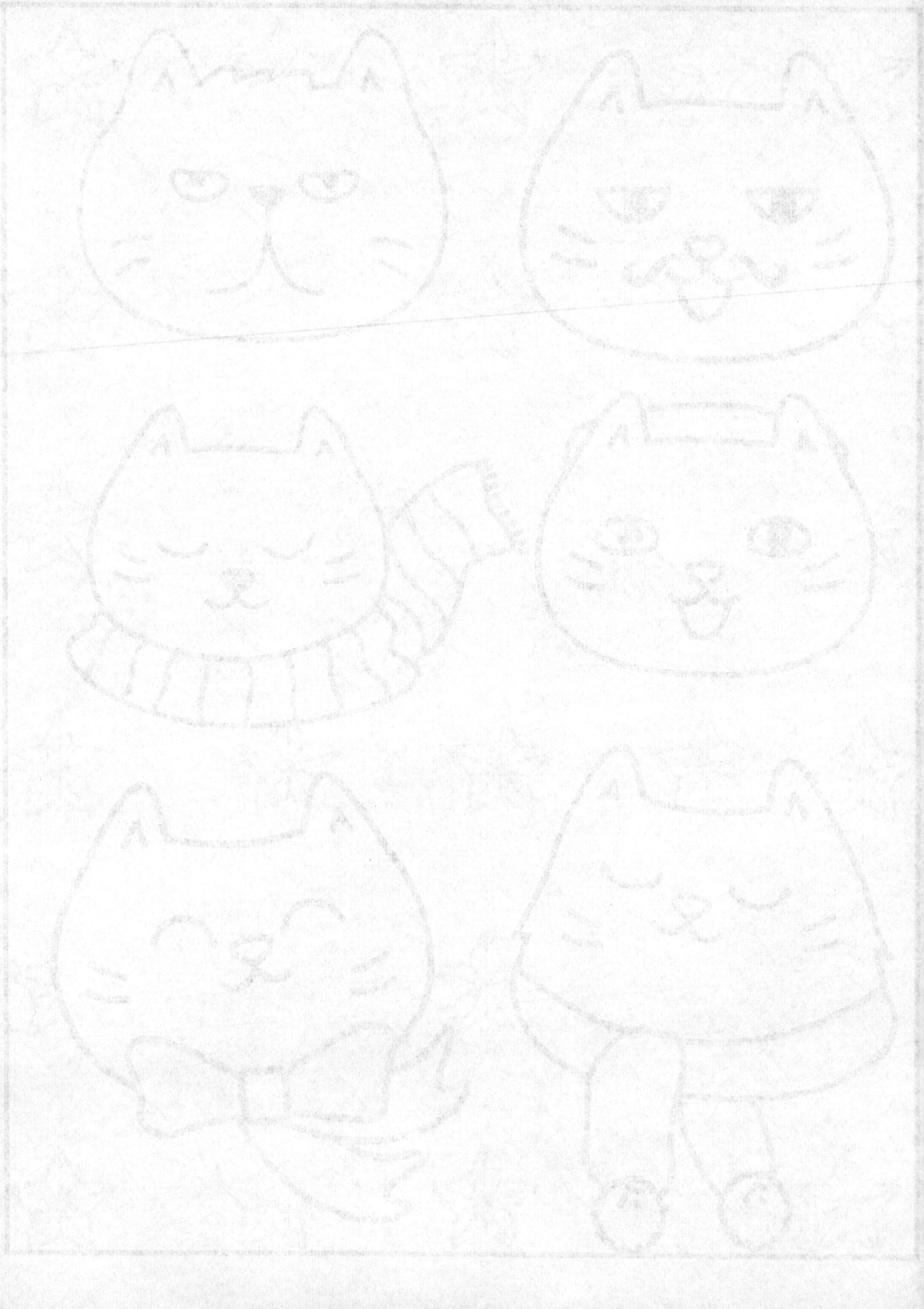

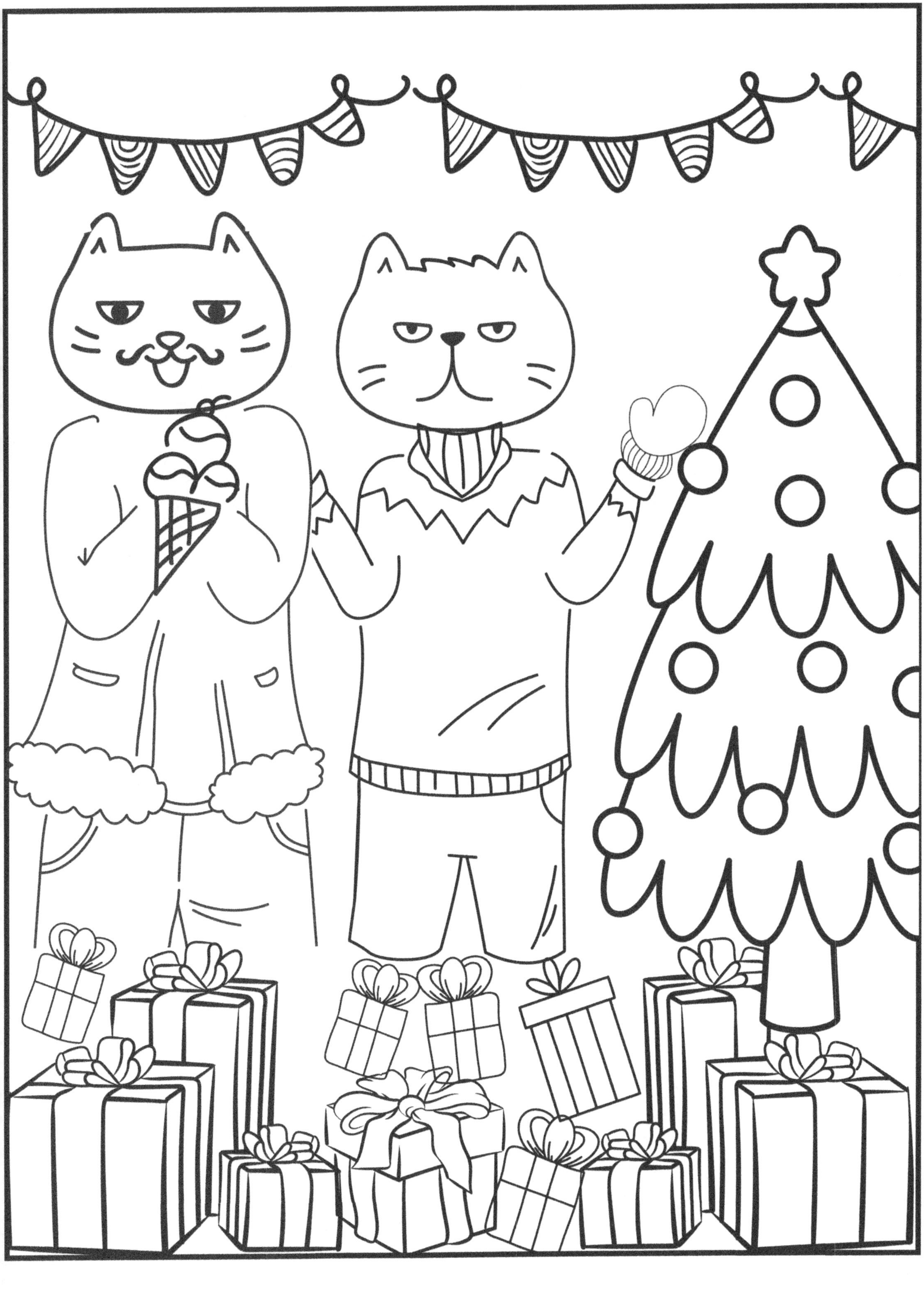

Made in United States
North Haven, CT
23 November 2024

60817095R00046